TALKING TO THE DEAD

Also by George Noory

Worker in the Light
Journey to the Light

Also by Rosemary Ellen Guiley

The Encyclopedia of Ghosts and Spirits
The Encyclopedia of Angels
Ask the Angels
The Vengeful Djinn
(coauthor with Philip J. Imbrogno)

TALKING TO THE DEAD

George Noory

AND

Rosemary Ellen Guiley

A TOM DOHERTY ASSOCIATES BOOK

NEW YORK

TALKING TO THE DEAD

A Forge Book
Published by Tom Doherty Associates, LLC
175 Fifth Avenue
New York, NY 10010

www.tor-forge.com

Forge® is a registered trademark of Tom Doherty
Associates, LLC.

Library of Congress Cataloging-in-Publication Data

Noory, George.
　　Talking to the dead / George Noory and Rosemary Ellen
Guiley.—1
　　　　p. cm.
　　ISBN 978-0-7653-2538-9 (hardback)
　　1. Spiritualism—Fiction.　2. Supernatural—Fiction.
I. Guiley, Rosemary.　II. Title.
　　PS3614.O675T35 2011
　　813'.6—dc22

　　　　　　　　　　　　　　　　　　　　　　2011021564

First Edition: October 2011

Printed in the United States of America

0　9　8　7　6　5　4　3　2　1

Contents

CONTENTS

Acknowledgments

The research of many individuals and organizations went into this book, and in particular we would like to express special thanks for the help provided by Tom and Lisa Butler (codirectors of the Association for Transcommunication); Ron Ricketts; Philip J. Imbrogno; Mark Macy; Bill Chappell; Margaret Downey; Martha Copeland; Stephen Rorke; David M. Rountree; Craig Telesha; and April and Allen Slaughter.

In addition, I would like to thank my parents, Georgette and Gabriel; my two sisters, Gail and Glinda; and my trusting staff, Lisa Lyon, Tom Danheiser, Stephanie Smith, and Dan Galanti. They all had the faith.

—George Noory

TALKING TO THE DEAD

Into the Unknown

On *Coast to Coast AM*, I deal with every paranormal, supernatural, spiritual, and mystical topic imaginable. There are no boundaries or limits, and both my guests and callers push the edges on any given night. Of all the subjects we hit on, the question of life after death ranks right at the top. Most compelling of all are the frequent heartfelt testimonies of people who have been in contact with loved ones on the Other Side.

We have no scientific proof yet of the afterlife, but those who have had such experiences know deep within their hearts that the afterlife is real and that the people they love dearly are alive in that world. Still, those callers and experts have questions. "What is the afterlife like?" "Can we communicate regularly with the dead?" "Can we validate our communications and experiences?"

I share those questions and convictions. My own personal spiritual search has led me to the unshakable conclusion that we do not die. I am absolutely convinced that there is an afterlife and that we carry on in new ways after we are done on Earth. Thus, I have been intensely interested in the field of spirit communications and especially in the new technology that offers the potential of better and provable contact, not only with the dead but perhaps with other entities in other realms as well.

My coauthor, Rosemary Ellen Guiley, shares the same interests. Rosemary has been a frequent guest, not only on *Coast to Coast AM* but also on my old radio show in St. Louis, *Night Talk with the Night Hawk*. I met Rosemary, first over e-mail and on the air, in 1998. We did many shows on the meanings of dreams, including dreams of the dead. So many callers were certain they had had real visits from dead loved ones in their dreams, but they often questioned their feelings, for they had been conditioned to think of dreams as imaginary, not real, events. As we have discussed often on the air, back then in St. Louis and today on *Coast to Coast AM*, there is a long history of dream visitations. Dreams, it seems, are one of the communication methods most often used between the living and the dead.

Up until about the nineteenth century, dreams and human mediumship were our primary means of interworld communication. We occasionally used rather primitive devices, such as divination tools, to help the process. The nineteenth century ushered in the age of machines, and spirit communications were forever changed. In the century-plus since then, we have invented ever more effective and intriguing ways of using devices to establish communication with other realms.

Both Rosemary and I have followed these developments with great interest, and Rosemary has been experimenting with spirit communications devices in her general work in the paranormal. Spirit communications are the key to proving the afterlife, one of the greatest questions confronting humanity since our beginnings. In this book, we explore the newest, technological side of our attempts to link a bridge to the afterlife.

The developments in spirit communications over recent decades have been nothing short of astonishing. Whether you can accept the evidence or not, the results are impossible to dismiss. To us, the evidence is clear: we already have the tools for establishing real-time, two-way contact with the dead, as well as entities who perhaps live in parallel worlds to ours, and possibly even with versions of ourselves in parallel dimensions. This book focuses on exciting technological developments for talking to the dead. The field is constantly changing with new developments, not only involving the transmission of voices, but images as well.

Contact raises many questions: What are the implications of spirit communications, and their impact on our beliefs? Contact stands to change us, but how? What are the ethics and morals involved? How should we look at developing more technological advancements? What do we learn about the afterlife? Are there a heaven and a hell? What about reincarnation?

Spirit communications address all of these questions, and more. It is one of the most exciting fields in the paranormal. We hope that through this book you will share our passion for more exploration.

You may already be familiar with the term "Electronic Voice Phenomena" to describe unknown voices captured on tape and digital recordings (and even on film and videotape). "Electronic Voice Phenomena" has been joined by "Instrumental Transcommunication," a term applied to broader technological applications in spirit communications. Just about every high-tech communications device imaginable has been used or adapted for the purpose of penetrating other realms.

Those who communicate from the Other Side talk about the afterlife not so much in terms of "heaven" or "hell," but as a state—or states—of existence involving the astral plane. The astral plane, it seems, has different regions of positive and unpleasant conditions. It is as varied as the topography of Earth.

The material communicated by the dead and their spirit helpers will confirm some of your beliefs and will challenge others. Regardless, we believe you will be stimulated to learn more. The beauty of modern spirit communications is, the technology has advanced so that just about anybody can use a variety of devices for experimentation. We talk about that, too, and how you can pursue experiments on your own.

Our ability to communicate with the other side may involve portals and wormholes described in quantum physics, a topic we also address. So, open up the portals of your mind and engage in the biggest adventure of all—the exploration of life beyond death.

1

The Spirit World Is Calling

Nighttime radio is the perfect confessional. Every night as the host of *Coast to Coast AM*, I hear it all: meetings with the dead, out-of-body journeys, encounters with aliens and entities, prophetic dreams, miracles—you name it about the strange, we get it nightly.

One of the most popular topics that people cannot seem to hear enough about, or talk enough about, is contact with the dead. Almost everyone has a story about a time when they felt visited or contacted by someone who had passed over. Perhaps the experience was comforting; perhaps it was unsettling. Either way, it was definitely unforgettable, and maybe even life changing.

On this night, Rosemary Ellen Guiley has joined me in the studio in Sherman Oaks, California, to talk especially about communication with the dead and take calls on Open Lines. We both know it's going to be an active night. Some nights are just like that—you can feel a charge in the air, like the *Coast to Coast* audience has linked up in a peculiar, energized group mind. My producer, Tom Danheiser, can feel it, too. Tom screens the calls. Sometimes the phone lines are "hot" before we even start taking the calls.

After we talk for a few minutes about Rosemary's latest research in spirit communications, we open the lines. They are already full with people waiting to tell their stories about talking to the dead.

"Beth, east of the Rockies," I said to the first caller. "You're on the air."

"George?" Beth sounded hesitant.

"Go ahead, Beth; you're on the air."

"Yes, okay, thank you. I'm so glad you're doing this subject, and I want to tell you and Rosemary what happened to me." There is a brief pause, and we can almost hear Beth taking a big breath to plunge ahead on what must be a difficult topic.

Beth continued, "My dad died several years ago in a car accident. It was a big shock to everyone in our family, and"—her voice broke with emotion—"I had a hard time dealing with it." She took a moment to compose herself. "But here's the weird part: about three weeks after he was gone, I think he called me on the phone!"

Rosemary nods to me in the studio. We've both heard these types of stories many times.

"He called you on the phone?" I said to Beth. "Tell us what happened."

"I was at home by myself one day; it was in the afternoon. The phone rang and I thought it sounded strange. I mean, it didn't have its usual ring. It sounded kind of distorted. I thought maybe there was something going wrong with the line.

"When I picked up the receiver and said, 'Hello,' I could hear a lot of static. It reminded me of how long-distance calls used to sound, you know, like they were coming from very far away, with lots of interference on the line.

"I didn't hear any voices at first, and I said, 'Hello,' two or three times. And then this voice called out, 'Beth . . . Beth . . . is that you?' *And it sounded just like my dad!* I'm not making this up! I'd know his voice anywhere!"

"What did you say back?" I asked.

"I was so shocked I couldn't say anything. He repeated, 'Beth, is that you?' I said, 'Dad! Dad! Is that *you?*' I was practically shouting. He just repeated, 'Beth . . . Beth . . . Beth.' The static sound got worse and his voice got fainter and fainter and then it just stopped. I kept shouting into the phone for him to come back, but there was nothing but static, and then the line just went dead, like someone pulled the cord out of the wall. I hung up the phone and then picked it up again, and the dial tone was normal. I was pretty shook up for the rest of the day. In fact, I still am, if I think about it. I keep telling myself it was a fluke call, a wrong number, and it was a man who just sounded like my dad. But he called me by *name*."

"Rosemary, what do you make of this?" I said. "Do you think Beth might have really talked to her father—and he was calling from the Other Side?"

"It's quite possible," she answered. "There is a phenomenon literally called phone calls from the dead, or Anomalous Telephone Contacts, and it has been documented just about as long as the telephone has been in existence. Under certain circumstances, the dead seem to be able to access our phone technology and make calls to the living. Many of them are just like Beth described—they are full of static, but the voice of the dead person is recognizable, and it may just repeat a name or a phrase or sentence, almost in robot fashion. The calls either terminate abruptly or the voice simply fades away and the call ends. Most phone calls from the dead are very short—less than a minute—although a few longer ones have been documented, and I can think of one from the parapsychology literature that was reported to last about thirty minutes."

"Thirty minutes!" I said. "You mean someone could be talking to a dead person for half an hour and not know it?"

Rosemary laughed. "Well, in that case, the person had died and the recipient of the call didn't know it. She thought she was talking to someone who was still alive. Later she tried to call the person back, and was informed that the person had died before the call was made."

"That's amazing. Do we know how they can do this?"

I asked. "Do they just pick up a telephone on the Other Side and punch in our number?"

"No one really knows how it happens, or even why it happens," Rosemary said. "If it were easy to do, we would expect to see phone calls from the dead more often. Wishing for one does not seem to make a difference in terms of whether a person gets such a call or not. The barrier between the world of the living and the world of the dead is hard to penetrate. But it can be done, as we have seen throughout history, and the barrier is broken through every day. People have all kinds of experiences communicating with the dead, and increasingly so with technology."

"Let's go to first-time caller Wilma."

"Oh! I'm actually on the air?" said a startled voice.

"We're glad you can join us tonight. What's your question? Have you had a phone call from someone who has died?"

"I'm glad you're talking about this, George," said Wilma. "I don't know for certain, but I think my mother called me right after she died."

"Tell us what happened."

"Well, she had been sick for a long time—she had cancer. She was in the hospital, and we all knew she was going. It was just a matter of time. I never could sleep very well because I was always worried that I would get a call in the middle of the night. That's exactly what happened, but it wasn't the hospital calling. The phone rang a few minutes before three in the morning—I remember because I looked at the clock before I answered it. I said,

'Hello,' and heard this voice on the other end. It sounded like someone was trying to talk but was making only garbled sounds. There was a lot of static. I thought maybe I'd gotten a wrong number, so I hung up. Then a little while later my sister called. She had gotten a call from the hospital—she said Mom was gone. She died at about the same time that I got the call! I always thought that call was some sort of 'wake-up call,' if you know what I mean, to let me know Mom was going. But listening to your topic tonight, I'm wondering if it was Mom herself?"

"Rosemary?"

"Here again the evidence points to it being possible," she said. "Wilma has plenty of company. We have a long history of documented experiences in which people who are dying or who have just died communicate with the living—sort of a final farewell. Sometimes the living get what we call a 'crisis apparition,' a vision of the dead person. In other cases, it seems that technology is the easiest way to make a connection, and we get a mysterious phone call. We don't know how it happens, or why it only happens in certain cases—but it seems the dead can call us on the phone when the conditions are right."

"If I had stayed on the line, would she have been able to talk to me?" Wilma asked. We could hear the distress in her voice that she might have missed an opportunity to talk to her mother one last time.

"That was probably the best that could come through," Rosemary said. "These calls don't seem to last very long, a few seconds. It's amazing that they happen at all. If you had stayed on the line, the call probably would have either ended abruptly or just faded away."

"I suppose if the dead could call us easily on the phone, we would have more of these calls," I said. "How common is this? Do a lot of people get phone calls from the dead?"

"More than most people might think," Rosemary answered.

"But how do we really know we are talking to the dead and it's not just our imagination—or some cosmic trickster playing a joke on us?"

"We have to rely on the testimony of witnesses," Rosemary said. "The record is very convincing. There is quite a bit of evidence that we have been getting mysterious communications ever since the telephone was invented, and even before that, in Morse code. In the 1960s, two paranormal researchers, D. Scott Rogo and Raymond Bayless, heard about phone calls from the dead and were quite skeptical about them. They investigated, collected dozens of cases— and concluded that these calls are genuine. They published their documentation in *Phone Calls from the Dead*."

"Does the kind of phone matter?" I asked. "Does it have to be a conventional landline—or can we get phone calls from the dead on our cell phones?"

"Cell phones work, too," Rosemary answered. "It seems that both sides of the veil keep up with technology! In 2008 there was an interesting report on the news, about a man who was among those killed in a train accident in California. An autopsy revealed he had died instantly. But for some eleven hours after the crash was reported, several members of his family received more than thirty calls from his cell phone, which of course had caller ID. The calls consisted of static and noises. They thought he was alive and perhaps buried under the wreckage, unable to speak. It's hard to explain away all those calls as fluke random dials of his phone address book. The calls were targeted to members of his family, including his fiancée—not to business contacts."

"Rosemary, we've just gotten an e-mail from a listener named Andy, who says that he got a call on his cell phone from a friend of his who was dead. The call came on the anniversary of the friend's death."

"Anniversaries of someone's death evoke a lot of emotions," Rosemary observed. "Intense emotions seem to be a major factor in our ability to have contact with the dead. They don't guarantee contact, but they are important in a mix of factors that researchers are trying to understand and document. The evidence for contact is out there."

"We have certainly been hearing some interesting stories from our callers tonight," I said. "Let's go to another one. Tim, west of the Rockies. You're on."

"Hi, George, hi, Rosemary." Tim sounded enthusiastic. "A couple of things . . . One, I want to second what your other callers have said. I have never gotten a phone call from a dead person, but I do believe it can happen. I've done research on it."

"Have you had some other kind of contact with the dead, Tim?" I said.

"Yes, that's what I wanted to say, too. I started experimenting with Electronic Voice Phenomena and I have gotten lots of messages from the dead."

"Electronic Voice Phenomena, let's explain that for those who aren't familiar with it," I said. "Electronic Voice Phenomena. That is where you ask questions with a recorder on and perhaps there are answers on playback. Rosemary?"

"That's right, George. You don't actually hear the answers while you are recording, but they are there on playback. Here again, nobody knows exactly how or why it happens, but it has been documented by many researchers for nearly a century now. Anyone can do Electronic Voice Phenomena in any location. Some people record at home and other people record at haunted locations."

I went back to our caller: "So tell us about your messages, Tim. What do you get, and who are you talking to?"

"First I should tell you that I got interested in Electronic Voice Phenomena after I read about it," Tim said. "It sounded far-fetched to me, so I decided to give it a try, almost to prove to myself that there was nothing to it. I got a recorder out one night at home and asked a few questions, like, 'Is there anyone here who will talk to me,' 'tell me your name,' things like that. When you ask a question, you leave a little space of a few seconds for an answer. I didn't hear a thing with my ears, but when I played it back, after the question 'Is there anyone here who will talk to me?' a male voice said, 'Yes.' It was very clear. I nearly freaked out. I thought, *No way!*"

"Do you know who it was?" I asked.

"I'm not sure, but I think it might be my dead grand-father. He didn't give a name the first time, but I tried again the next night, and when I asked for the name of the man who had said, 'Yes,' it came back 'Emerson.' That was my grandfather's last name. He also said, 'Indiana,' and that's where he lived."

"Was it his voice?"

"He died before I was born, so I don't know."

"Have you asked anyone in your family to listen?"

"Not yet," Tim admitted. "I'm not sure they would be-lieve it." He paused and then added emphatically, "But *I* do."

"Rosemary, what do you think?"

"Sounds like Tim really did get some unexplained an-swers. Electronic Voice Phenomena are quite common and probably our biggest means of communicating with the dead, especially with technology," she said. "I've gotten lots of Electronic Voice Phenomena I can't explain. Sometimes we never know exactly who is communicating—they don't give a name or other identifying information. Maybe they just want to drop in and let us know that they're around. People who do Electronic Voice Phenomena regularly can build up exchanges with regular communicators. But a lot of messages are one-offs."

"You know, Rosemary, we've talked before about dreams of the dead and visits from the dead. That's how you and I met—I found your *Encyclopedia of Dreams* in a bookstore over ten years ago, when I had my nighttime show in St. Louis. One of the things that intrigued me the most about dreams was, can the dead really come to us while we are dreaming? It seems the dead can also make use of our technology for other kinds of communication, too."

"I believe they can and do," Rosemary said. "That's where the big excitement is in research. I've devoted a great deal of time to researching communication with the dead, and I conduct a lot of experiments with a variety of devices. I have had live exchanges that I cannot explain naturally."

"This is an area that we are going to have to explore in more depth," I said. "A lot of our callers have reported getting messages from the dead, not just by phone, but on recorders, in photographs and videos, even on their computer screens. Maybe the gates between the worlds are opening up."

"I am convinced they are, George. My prediction is that in the future—maybe the very near future—we will have the technology to talk with the dead whenever we or they want. And perhaps even talk to other entities. There is already evidence that we can do both. And we can do it in real-time, live, two-way communication."

"You mean talking to the dead or spirits like we are talking here tonight?" I asked.

"Absolutely. It can be done. Research has gone on for decades now in real-time Electronic Voice Phenomena, and some of the evidence is staggering. I have several of these communication devices myself. They go by different names, like ghost boxes, Frank's Boxes, MiniBoxes. The more I use them, the more I am convinced we can break through interdimensional barriers."

"Where do you get these devices?"

"They are made by independent researchers, who usually

have backgrounds in electronics, electrical engineering, computers, and science. Some are available commercially. So anyone potentially can get or make one and start experimenting with it."

"Let's bring some into the studio," I suggested.

"I can do that. And I have some interesting clips to play of communication exchanges I have had that I believe come from another realm."

The night went on with many more intriguing calls and personal stories. And that's how this book was born. The two of us had had many conversations on air and off the air about spirit communications, the inevitable development of technology to make real-time spirit communications possible—and the ramifications for all of us in terms of learning the truth about the Other Side, and how it might affect our personal, religious, social, and even political views. There is a lot more at stake in spirit communications than getting a comforting message that a dead loved one is all right.

More and more, the dead are speaking out. They want us to listen, and they are finding ways to use our technology to reach us. My and Rosemary's research took us into amazing territory, and in the following pages we share our findings, our thoughts, and our vision with you.

It was clear to me that our communications technology has vaulted us into a brave new world of interdimensional contact. People all over the world have been experimenting with Electronic Voice Phenomena for decades. Now these real-time Electronic Voice Phenomena bring a whole new dimension to our search for proof of the afterlife.

Actually, real-time Electronic Voice Phenomena have been around for a long time, too, but until a few years ago had not been available to the average person. Did you know that you, or anyone, can make or acquire a device that may open the door to the Other Side? Now here's the big question: if you could open that door, would you?

"I would definitely talk with the dead," said a caller named Ben one night on Open Lines. "I'd like to know what they're doing over there."

"Do you think they might be sitting down to a cheeseburger like us, or is it all harps and angels?" I commented.

"I don't know, but I can think of a few people who might be in for a barbecue instead," Ben said.

"You mean they're the ones in for a roasting."

"Something like that," Ben said with a laugh.

"We won't ask you who those people are. But seriously, Ben, why do you want to talk to someone who is dead? Maybe we should just leave well enough alone once a person has died."

"I want to know what the afterlife is like," Ben said. "I want to hear it with my own ears, from someone who is *there*."

On her next trip to Los Angeles, Rosemary brought several of her "real-time EVP" devices. She had been experimenting with them for several years. I wanted to see for myself if it is indeed possible to talk to the dead "on demand." Even though I was prepared, I was still surprised at what I heard. It's one thing to hear mystery voices on playback on a recorder—it's another to actually hear them real-time, as though a "live" person is talking, and to *you*.

We got together before air time, and Rosemary showed me how the devices work. Each one looked different, as they were all made by hand—but they all did the same thing: rapidly scan the AM radio band. Several were made by a man named Frank Sumption, who lives in Colorado and began making real-time "boxes," as they are called, after he became interested in Electronic Voice Phenomena. Sumption's work caught the attention of the paranormal investigation community. Other individuals built their own boxes, which became known in the paranormal jargon as "Frank's Boxes" and "ghost boxes." Ghost boxes isn't a very good name for them, but it has stuck for lack of a better term.

The scan rates of the AM radio bands can be adjusted manually. When the boxes are turned on and scanning, jumbles of words and sounds spilling out of them, it's hard not to feel a rush of excitement at the prospect of tuning in somehow to another world. The feeling must be similar to the excitement felt by the early pioneers of ordinary radio who clustered around their primitive sets trying to catch a live broadcast emanating from some distant place on the planet. Now technology can turn the ordinary citizen into a SETI (Search for Extraterrestrial Intelligence) pioneer of sorts, listening for voices emanating from beyond the planet and beyond life as we know it.

It just makes shivers go up and down your spine.

Rosemary turned on one of her newer devices, called a "MiniBox," which had become her favorite. It was created by a Texan named Ron Ricketts. It was a small black plastic box with an assortment of lights and knobs. When it was turned on, a cacophony of noise erupted. It was like listening to a global party phone line or a large number of radio stations all playing at once. The MiniBox scanned like a busy bee, lighting on a station for a second or two, then zooming on to the next. We could hear words, notes of music, bursts of static, and so on.

"Why do we need all that noise?" I asked.

"In order to talk to us, those in another dimension seem to do best when we give them a background of sounds. They're not using the vocal cords of the living. We've asked communicators how they speak, and they say that they manipulate energy on their side and sound on ours. It's a process we do not yet fully understand—but it happens. You could liken it to needing paper or canvas in order to paint a picture."

"How do you know when you've gotten an answer?" I said, trying to focus in on the rush of sounds.

"Sometimes words do pop out of broadcasts that seem to be answers to questions, and some people feel that they are evidential, based on the odds of timing. But the best are voices that are clearly not part of a radio broadcast—they are talking directly to you, over and above the scan noise. They ride in on a separate signal. It's like being in a crowd, talking against a background of noise. Sometimes the voices are loud and clear, and other times they are faint.

Real-time EVP voices are like recorded EVP voices—they have strange cadences, or they sound flat or even robotic. They do not sound like normal voices of the living."

Rosemary adjusted the settings on the MiniBox. "I usually start by identifying myself and others present, and asking if there are communicators who wish to speak with us. I ask for their names. I ask if they can tell us our names. I usually hear my name more than once in any given session. Rosemary is not a common name, and the odds of hearing it randomly on the radio, especially in direct response to a question, are very low."

She introduced us, stating our names. "Is anyone present who can speak to us through this device?" she asked. "Can you identify yourselves?"

All we heard was the smashed-up radio chatter.

"Usually it takes a few minutes to warm up," she said. "Sometimes I get something right away, as soon as I turn it on, even before I ask a question."

"Would anyone like to talk to me?" I ventured.

A few seconds went by, and then a tinny male voice said, "Hel-lo . . . George." It sounded like a voice rising up out of the depths and breaking the surface of the background racket.

I was electrified. "Who was that?"

"I don't know," Rosemary said. "Did you recognize the voice?"

I shook my head.

"Sometimes they don't give their names. It's often hard to hold a connection for more than a question or two. For one thing, the scan is constantly changing. It's probably because we have very primitive technology for this sort of interdimensional thing."

She addressed the MiniBox: "Who is talking to George?"

Again a few seconds went by. Then we heard, faintly, ". . . Ge-orge . . ." It sounded like a bad cell phone call breaking up.

We never did learn who that was, but it seemed that someone "out there," perhaps on the Other Side, had caught our transmission—and answered back. We asked other questions, and Rosemary asked if the communicators could tune in better to our device. A male voice answered, "We are trying." The words were jammed together in an odd cadence.

"I think we actually pick up only a portion of what is being transmitted to us," Rosemary said. "And maybe they hear only part of what we are saying."

I wanted to do a live demonstration of the boxes on that show that night, but we discovered that the shielding in the broadcast room, which eliminates interference, also prevented the devices from picking up outside radio stations and creating the background scanning noise. Still, we took the devices to the studio to talk about them.

Rosemary set them up and we got ready to go on air. After my news announcements, I introduced our first topic of spirit communications.

"Imagine being able to pick up a phone, or a device like it, and dial up the Other Side. Answering on the Other Side is someone who is no longer of this world—they're dead. Now, does that sound way far-fetched? Not in the eyes of researchers all over the world who are now pursuing technical links with other realms for real-time two-way communication. Rosemary Ellen Guiley is live in the studio, and has got some of these devices with her."

"These boxes are a type of device intended to get real-time, two-way communication with the dead and other beings," Rosemary explained. "They scan the AM radio band and create a noise matrix that, the theory goes, spirits can manipulate to make words, sort of like an audible clay. The scan is rapid, so that you're only getting a word or two or brief sound as each station is passed. Communications that are considered unexplained are phrases or sentences that extend over multiple stations—they in effect ride on top of the scan. This is part of a field of research called 'Instrumental Transcommunications.'"

"Is this similar to what Thomas Edison was trying to develop before he died?" I asked.

"Word has it that Edison was interested in making a device or telephone for talking to the dead," Rosemary said. "Whether he actually worked on such a device is not known, and the evidence for it is controversial. But he certainly had an interest in it."

"Some researchers say they get their advice and instructions for making these devices from the dead themselves. Is that possible?"

"It seems to be the case," she replied. "Some inventors of these devices say they communicate with the dead, and others say they are in contact with higher beings called ethereals, who might be likened to angels. These beings provide inspiration and sometimes technical information."

"Do they give schematics? How do they communicate?"

"In a variety of ways. Sometimes through regular Electronic Voice Phenomena, sometimes through dreams, and sometimes in inspiration—ideas that just fall into people's heads."

"Assuming these are sounds from the Other Side, that tells me there is something truly scientific going on," I commented. "It seems normal to think that as we speak here, they also speak over there. These devices have the ability to pick it up, like a dog that hears things we can't."

"That's the idea," Rosemary agreed. "Our attempts at spirit communication go back to ancient times. The tools and technology have changed—simple devices that we see as quite primitive today were considered high tech in their times. Now we are experimenting in spirit communications in the age of electronic media. We've improved our equipment and we are able to tune into the subtle vibrations of these realms better."

"All right, let's go to our first-time caller line. Hello!"

"Hello," a woman's voice said. ". . . are you talking to me?"

"Yes—you sound like an EVP voice yourself," I joked.

She laughed. "I just wanted to say, quite a while back a man called in. He had bought an inexpensive radio and he said either at the top or bottom of the dial he picked up his dead mother talking to him."

"I remember that call—you've got a great memory.

Rosemary? Can we pick up voices of the dead with ordinary radios?"

"Yes, people have gotten mysterious voices over all sorts of devices. The ghost boxes are specially designed to improve our chances, especially for communication on demand."

"How reliable is it? Can we ask for someone in particular?"

"You can, but you never know what you're going to get," she said. "It's also hard to have sustained conversations, because each scan of the radio band is never exactly the same. We have a long way to go before it's like talking on the phone today. But the results show we can do it."

The next caller was a man who suggested that a ghost box be taken to the Hollywood Roosevelt Hotel, reputed to be haunted by the ghost of Marilyn Monroe. Maybe someone could talk to her and find out what really happened to her when she died, he said.

"That's an interesting idea," I said. "Maybe we could solve all sorts of mystery deaths and disappearances."

"I like to take my devices into haunted locations," Rosemary said. "If we went to the Roosevelt, would we get Marilyn Monroe on the other end? Who knows—but there is always the chance of learning something that could be investigated and verified."

"How should these devices be used?" I asked. "Is it a good idea to put these devices into the hands of people who may not know what they're doing?"

"There is always a dark shadow side. Anything can be misused. You can't police how it is going to be used and how it might affect someone. But it's good to have as many of these devices as possible; it makes it possible to run experiments, especially if we have devices with standard designs."

"Let's go east of the Rockies. Welcome to *Coast to Coast*, you're on the air. What's your name?"

"My name is Jack and I'm calling from Kentucky."

"Go ahead, Jack."

"I've been in the paranormal for about fifteen years and I've experimented with listening between the lines in AM radio, if you know what I mean, and also Electronic Voice Phenomena. What is the danger in dabbling with the voices of the disembodied and things of that nature? It seems to me that you could possibly let things in that might cause some problems."

"Rosemary, how do we know that these disembodied entities who talk to us aren't tricking us into giving them a key to this side?"

"It is difficult if not impossible to always prove the identity of communicators," she said. "It is a hazard. But there are hazards to exploring any frontier."

"Centuries ago, people were afraid to sail very far into the ocean because they thought it was full of sea monsters—or they were convinced they would fall off the edge of the flat Earth," I said.

"And they had to just do it and keep doing it to demonstrate otherwise," Rosemary added. "We do have to use discernment and care in working with spirit communications devices. But the benefits to making a big breakthrough far outweigh the hazards."

"I can think of a lot of benefits," I said. "Proving we do survive after death, helping grief, learning new information that would influence science and technology."

"There is a big potential payoff, if we can improve our technology and validate our results."

Later on, as Rosemary and I got deeper into our research of spirit communications, we found that there are quite a few people who think that talking to the dead is not automatically a great idea. Just about everyone says they would like to know for certain that there is an afterlife—but what if we find out information we would rather not know? Despite these concerns, my and Rosemary's research convinced us that all of us on the planet stand to benefit by having reliable contact with the Other Side, and also potentially with nonhuman entities who live in other realms as well.

Does it sound like science fiction? It's already more real than you might imagine. An astounding amount of high-tech research has gone on for more than a century, and there are people all over the planet who take talking to the dead for granted—because they have been doing it for years.

"I want to delve into this as deeply as possible," I told Rosemary after the show. "I want to know about the whole history of high-tech spirit communications. But right now, I want to know more about these real-time EVP devices."

"The timing couldn't be better," she said with a smile. "I'm about to go to Dallas to meet Ron Ricketts, the inventor of the MiniBox. I'm going to ask him to try to explain the mystery behind them."

2

The Ghost in the Cosmic Box

One morning, Texas paranormal investigators April and Allen Slaughter got up and started their day. But instead of turning on the television or the radio like many people, they turned on their new MiniBox to see who might talk from the Other Side. After a short burst of static and the jumbled sounds of AM stations, a stadium-style voice boomed out, "Rose-mary El-len Gui-ley!"

Rosemary was not on the air that day in the Dallas–Fort Worth Metroplex, nor was she even in the area—she was twelve hundred miles away in Maryland. Her name was significant to the Slaughters. Not only were they all friends, but they were also all involved in the latest frontier in paranormal investigation, real-time, two-way EVP research. Was someone on the Other Side trying to get a message to the Slaughters about Rosemary or a message to Rosemary, who was soon to arrive? No further information came out, and the Slaughters concluded the communication was to get attention and alert them that those watching from the Other Side are aware of our plans and activities.

Before the MiniBox, there was Frank's Box.

Few people, including paranormal investigators, ever heard of MiniBoxes, Frank's Boxes, or ghost boxes prior to about 2004. That changed with Frank Sumption, a ham radio operator and electronics expert from Colorado. In 1995 Sumption read an article on Electronic Voice Phenomena in *Popular Electronics* and decided to give it a try. One trial yielded no results, and Sumption set the magazine aside and thought perhaps he would try it again at a later date. Four years went by, and around Christmastime 1999 Sumption chanced across the magazine and decided it was time to experiment again. This time, he tried Electronic Voice Phenomena using white noise as a background. He captured several voices, including that of an old man who sounded familiar to Sumption. From then on, Sumption was hooked on Electronic Voice Phenomena and he began to tinker in his basement workshop with various ways to improve methods of recording, including software designed to aid Electronic Voice Phenomena.

After months of recording, Sumption noticed that some of the messages he received were relayed to him by spirits who could use computer software and who acted on behalf of other communicators who could not. That set him wondering about other ways to reach all kinds of communicators. The intention turned in his mind for a week or so, and then suddenly an idea for a device crystallized. Sumption saw it complete in his head—all he had to do was build it from digital car stereos and other spare parts. The first "Frank's Box" was born in the summer of 2002. The device used white noise that amplified, filtered, and rectified to provide a random voltage to tune voltage-tunable radio receiver modules that were removed from older digital car stereos, as Sumption described. The randomly tuned radio modules provided a source of audio that was sent to an enclosure called an echo box. Essentially, what Frank's Box did was randomly scan radio frequencies, producing bits and fragments of speech and sound, with Electronic Voice Phenomena overlaid on top of it. The sweep seemed to produce better Electronic Voice Phenomena than white noise with an audio recorder. Some of the Electronic Voice Phenomena were live, and some were passive, heard after the fact on recordings, much like standard Electronic Voice Phenomena.

Sumption kept tinkering and making improvements, trying both AM and FM, using his devices for his own experiments. Some of his communicators identified themselves as extraterrestrials, implying that the dead on the Other Side may not be the only ones who can come through.

Sumption originally did not intend his Frank's Boxes

to be used for paranormal investigation, but he gave a few to an investigator for testing and soon others were fascinated by the possibilities offered by the boxes.

Rosemary first saw a demonstration of a Frank's Box at a paranormal conference. The bizarre and exotic sounds of the sweep itself seemed to penetrate an interdimensional veil. Looking around at the large crowd assembled for the demonstration, she saw how riveted everyone was over the prospect of hearing live voices of the dead. The emotional intensity rivaled that of a religious revival. Some people had tears flowing down their cheeks. Some were so overcome they had to leave the room. Others had skeptical expressions on their faces but were nonetheless listening with great interest.

Lots had been drawn for a few opportunities to personally ask questions through the box. Some of those persons went away convinced they had heard recognizable voices of loved ones on the Other Side. But not everyone thought the box was the real deal—questions and doubts circulated in the post-event conversations.

Word about Frank's Boxes spread around the paranormal community. Many people wanted to get one, but Sumption was not producing them commercially. Each one was handmade from spare parts. The small number of them and the fact that they were not commercially produced made them highly desirable. Rosemary acquired four of these from Sumption, numbered 22, 23, 45, and 54. April and Allen Slaughter acquired several as well.

Sumption published his schematics on the Internet,

which aided other inventors in creating their own versions of ghost boxes, including easy modifications of existing commercial radios. Ghost boxes took their place as a tool for paranormal investigation and for personal use. Though some people used them for entertainment, others had communications experiences beyond their expectations— from the mundane into the mystical.

Rosemary started taking a ghost box on most of her paranormal investigations, figuring that haunted locations might be good prospects for significant results with their active phenomena. Spirit communications can in fact be obtained anywhere, even in your own home.

Ron Ricketts never expected to become involved in spirit communications, let alone make them. Call it fate, call it destiny, but some higher forces were at work to draw him into the field. He created a standard design with a printed circuit board and rechargeable gel battery; more advanced models had internal memory and multiple types of sweeps. Rosemary obtained the first available MiniBox in 2007 and it immediately became her favorite. Small and compact, it offered advantages for travel.

Rosemary met up with Ricketts at the Slaughters' home, and their evening included some work with new MiniBoxes he had brought along. Ricketts has been self-employed in the electronics, engineering, and computer fields since 1980. His educational background is in geology and chemistry, and he has put in more than forty years as a ham radio operator. Like most people who are drawn to the paranormal, he had some pivotal experiences early in life, including growing up in a haunted house with a history tailor-made for a horror film. At age eleven in 1959, Ricketts obtained a tape recorder and decided to try to catch the voices of the dead.

"We lived in a Civil War–era home that had been a funeral parlor," he related. "Three stories plus a full basement. The basement was always creepy and my mother didn't like going down there. One night I was home alone and out of nowhere I got this outlandish idea—I think it was inspired. We had a huge brick fireplace with a little grate that had a chute for pouring ashes down to the basement to a collecting bin, in what had been the old funeral parlor's preparation room. I had a very long microphone cord. The idea came full-blown into my head that I could lower the microphone all the way down to the other side of the bin, where all the dead bodies used to be, and maybe the dead would talk to me. I recorded about thirty minutes of reel-to-reel tape. When I listened to it, I heard muffled moans and sounds like words. It was so creepy that I didn't tell my mom or dad. I wiped over the tape."

Another significant experience, this time with something much darker, occurred when Ricketts was about eighteen: "I had a buddy who told me that a man had hung himself the night before in the restroom in an old park in the dilapidated part of town. He said the body had just been removed and suggested that we go over to check the place out. I had my intended bride-to-be with me. She stayed in the car while my friend and I walked toward the men's room. As we got near the door, a boiling black mass poured out and came swirling directly toward us! We immediately did a 'Dude, run!' straight back for the car.

"I turned around once and I could see this black swirling tornado with a tail on it. I didn't know what it was, but it was black as ink. My friend made a head-first dive into the backseat window and I jumped into the driver's seat. We tore out of there like all get-out. It wasn't until years later that I realized I had encountered my first malignant materialization."

The negativity of the entity didn't deter Ricketts from delving deeper into the paranormal. He remained fascinated by it. "That experience got me reading books about hauntings, entities, and UFOs," he said. "I'd had other smaller things happen to me when I was a child. I've been reading and studying ever since. By the time I got to my thirties I realized there was some underlying structure to all of this and that it had to be interrelated. I found Jacques Vallee's *Passport to Magonia*, which ties the supernatural all together. Then I discovered John Keel, Allen Hynek, Stanton Friedman, and others. I joined MUFON (the Mutual UFO Network) and APRO (the now-defunct Aerial Phenomena Research Organization), and I knew the APRO founders, Jimmy and Coral Lorenzen."

Ricketts' years of immersion in various aspects of the paranormal created an ideal background for spirit communications. However, he might never have become involved in the field had it not been for Sumption.

"I give all credit to Frank," Ricketts told Rosemary. "He is the individual with the seminal idea that got this whole box thing going."

In the fall of 2006, Ricketts was a member of a paranormal investigation group called the Denton Area Paranormal Society, run by Lance Oliver. One day Oliver came to Ricketts and asked him if he'd ever heard of a Frank's Box and could he build one. Ricketts did some research and came away quite skeptical—he did not see how sweeping the radio band would enable discarnate entities to communicate. He told Oliver he wasn't going to waste his time building such a device.

In the summer of 2007, Ricketts joined another paranormal organization. The director, Rick Moran, was also interested in acquiring a Frank's Box and asked Ricketts to build one. Again Ricketts declined, but Moran persuaded him to change his mind.

"Almost thirty days later I had a prototype sitting on Rick's kitchen table," Ricketts recalled. "The box called his name several times, and he talked to his deceased daughter. I knew then it was going to work. I was actually disturbed by this. I come from a very strong engineering background—I'm an empiricist and a theorist, but I have an open mind as well. I was running into a major conflict. My engineer side said that I know every transistor, every amp, everything that's inside this device. There is nothing magic in there, nothing that has been blessed by the gods. It is nothing more than a machine. And yet it calls me by name, it says things to me that are true, and in my presence it has come out in the voice of the deceased daughter of someone I know. I was wondering if I was losing my mind.

"I've been a radio amateur for over forty years, and I've spent countless thousands of hours scanning the radio bands, every frequency you can imagine, all the way from DC to daylight. Other than a few odd things I've heard along the way, I had never heard anything like this."

Moran asked Ricketts to build more and suggested that he sell them. Ricketts wasn't sure he should do that: "I felt like Oppenheimer when he realized he had the atom bomb. I've got something here that logic tells me cannot work, and yet it apparently works. And not just for me. Everyone who sat down with the box, within a matter of minutes, had it start calling them by name. It answered their questions and told them things that only they knew. I wondered, *What are the implications of releasing this to the public?*"

After a week of thought, Ricketts concluded that any potential problems resided with how the device was used, not with the device itself. He decided to make more, but with the caveat that no claims would be made as to what the box does or who communicates through it. The Mini-Box was officially born.

A month later, April Slaughter took Ricketts' prototype to a paranormal event at The Stanley Hotel in Estes Park, Colorado. Rosemary was there, too. The MiniBox created a sensation. April and Rosemary gave individual demonstrations to Mark Macy, a leading researcher in spirit communications; Frank Sumption; and others. Everyone was impressed.

Rosemary asked Ricketts how the box works to connect different worlds.

"There are roughly three things at work in equal measure when it comes to interpreting the voices," Ricketts said. "The first level is wishful thinking. People listen to the MiniBox and hear a jumble of radio stations. They concentrate on the words that pop out and grab onto them. They hear what they want to hear, and it makes them happy. But that is not what the *box* is saying.

"Some people never get beyond that level. Once you get used to the box, you can move on to the second level of communication, which is hearing words clearly that are not part of the radio broadcast. Out of thin air, someone says a word or phrase that is germane to your question, or is personal to you. You tune out the jumbles and chatter of the deejays—that's the crashing of the waves, so to speak. The unknown voices come from beneath the waves.

"Then there is a third level." Ricketts paused and smiled. "This is where I might lose a few people. You hear the box and you get a message *directly in your head* that is not audible but is impressed into your mind. This happens after you've been using the box a long time and you're in tune with it. The first few times it happens it scares you, but now you understand and the box is *really* working."

"I have experienced this myself," Rosemary told Ricketts. "There are occasional responses that seem to come from a word or two from radio broadcasts. If they occur quickly after a question is asked and have a direct bearing on the question, I give them some weight. Much better are responses that are too long to come from any one station due to the speed of the scan. These 'float' on top of the radio noise. The voices are like many I hear in traditional Electronic Voice Phenomena; that is, they sound flat and tinny, and are oddly modulated. Some communication I get is psychically or mentally in my head. Other people don't hear it, but I do. Other researchers have told me they have experienced this effect, too. It's evident to me that the box taps into levels of consciousness and processes that we don't understand. We shouldn't ignore or discard these mental results but instead study them to learn exactly what happens."

Ricketts nodded. "The box may actually work as some sort of channeling device, helping people with psychic or mediumistic ability to tune in better," he said.

"We've seen that people with natural mediumistic ability get the best results—although anyone can get at least some results," she said. "The box might help people tune in their own ability. The more I use one, the better it seems to work."

"The owner of a box imprints his or her energy on it by using it," Ricketts concurred. "I think that has a lot to do with how the box performs. You don't necessarily need to be psychic, either. An unskilled person with a good attitude can learn to use the box in ten minutes and be proficient in an hour. There are some people who, when they first turn it on, you can tell they are dang near level three. For people who are mediumistic, it seems to work in conjunction with their abilities rather than replace or overpower them. But having psychic ability doesn't seem to be a requirement—it does open up to people who are not talented in that area."

"I also feel the box is like a beacon," Rosemary said. "It sends out a signal into the ethers that is noticed by entities. They can home in on it to attempt communication."

Ricketts acknowledged he has had an uncanny sensitivity to the box, but he termed it "interesting" and not necessarily "psychic." "Fate decreed that I would make these boxes. I didn't go looking for them. I have untold thousands of hours listening to the MiniBox—probably have more box time than anybody alive. But I have less *communication* than anybody alive. I build it; I make sure its heart beats. I make sure it works. But I don't *use* the Mini-Box. I don't ask it questions and I don't listen to it, other than to make sure it is doing what it is supposed to do. I don't know why, but I have been adjured not to use it. It's a command that's been with me from Day One.

"When I make a new box and turn it on for the first time, I can tell by how it talks to me in the first ten seconds whether it will be a good box. I cannot tell you why I know this, but it is something I know as certain as my name. If the box is good, I turn the volume all the way down and set it aside. The next day, I turn it on and turn the volume up. If it still feels right, then it goes into a box ready for its new owner. I don't ask anything of it. I don't want it to tell me about the stock market or the winning lottery numbers. I feel like I am the watchmaker, and so I leave the divination to other people. That's the only way I can maintain my integrity—I have integrity with the box if I don't use it.

"So, I don't question any of my new children when I bring them to life. I can tell how they come up with their first cry if they are going to be a good child or a bad child. If they are going to be a bad child, I dispose of them. I break the circuit board in half and it goes in the trash. I don't salvage components, but I will reuse the box casing and the battery. There have been more than a few that have been thrown on the junk heap and scrapped after I finished building them."

"What makes a box inherently 'bad'?" Rosemary wanted to know.

"I actually don't know," Ricketts answered. "Again, it's a gut feeling I have. To paraphrase Stephen King, some places are born bad. Maybe some things are born bad, too. I had one that I turned on and the first thing it said was, 'F—— you.' I broke the board in half and threw it in the trash and said back, 'F——*you*.'"

The same sensitivity also tells Ricketts whether or not a box session will be productive: "I can tell within five seconds if it's going to be a good session, a bad session, or no session. Generally I don't participate; I just listen. That's in part self-defense. In the beginning, I was accused of fakery. Once I received a crank e-mail asking that, if the box was so wonderful, would it tune a television? I replied: 'If you buy the extra options it will even wash your dishes!'

Anway, I always let someone else run the box and I keep myself out of the loop so the box will pass or fail on its own merits."

External entities and forces also affect a session. Sometimes it is a no-go. "The box will tell you so," said Ricketts. "It will say, 'Go home,' 'Turn it off,' 'Shut me off.' When you hear that, the game is over—there is no point in trying more."

Once Ricketts was part of a team that was clearing a negative entity from a house and the MiniBox was employed in an attempt to communicate with it. "No box," came the emphatic statement, and the box immediately quit working, producing only static and occasional deejay chatter. When the entity was exorcized from the property, the box started working again.

Rosemary asked, "We have patterns now showing how the box works, and how it seems to interact with people. But *why* does it work?"

"I'm convinced that understanding how the box works is more vital than understanding any other aspect of this thing," he said. "I spend more time trying to figure out why it works than I do trying to invent new boxes. I'm trying to piece together a theory that fits everything together, and I'm looking at this as more than an engineer. We are looking at some kind of energy transfer that is not quantifiable in a normal manner. The box is almost like an open door. Understanding how this works will give us a peek into how underlying phenomena work as well.

"There is a fundamental mechanism at work that

transcends time and space. We are not talking about space brothers or men from Venus, Bigfoot or frogs falling from the sky, but about interdimensional collisions where the fabric of reality rips open briefly and someone looks through, or sticks their hand through, and then it shuts again. Actually, this is happening all the time, around us everywhere.

"Obviously a greater intelligence is at work. If people say to me that I don't believe in God, I say I believe in way more than God. I'm a very spiritual person, but I'm not a religious person. I envision a power and intelligence of the entire unbounded universe in all its dimensions. Now you're talking God!

"Somehow the box is a link to it all, this power and intelligence of everything that is out there. The box may be a microphone that anyone can walk up to and say, 'Howdy.' If we can figure out why the box works, it will lead to instrumentation for the next big step. We've got to get past the point where we treat these devices like novelties. The true scientific community is going to take a lot more convincing than anything we've come up with so far. That's what I want to do—find the answers. That's what people will write on my tombstone."

What Ricketts described as a rip in the fabric of reality corresponds to the descriptions of interdimensional reality employed centuries ago by alchemists. On the mundane level, alchemy is the search for a way to turn base metals such as lead into gold. But true alchemy is spiritual—the turning of the base metal of ordinary consciousness into the gold of spiritual enlightenment and ascension, the transcending of the need for physical form. The alchemist hopes to find the answers by accessing a rip in the fabric of the cosmos, called the *fenestra aeternitatis* or "window into eternity." The window is, in modern terms, a hole in the space-time continuum that enabled the alchemist to perceive the Unus Mundus, the All That Is.

Ricketts brought two new boxes with him to the Slaughters' home. After a dinner of fajitas, they all gathered back around the dining room table to try the boxes out. Ricketts had brought a MiniBox Plus for Rosemary, which featured programmable memory and fifteen modes of sweep. Inside the box was a quartz crystal wrapped in copper wire. Ricketts has an affinity with stones as well as machines and decided to add crystals to see if they improved results. April's box was a mediumistic prototype, with metal handles on the side. The operator holds the handles while the box is running, making a literal mind and body connection with the device itself.

Ricketts went over the MiniBox for Rosemary: "The new box works better in particular places. It has more scans, and you can save the scan. Everything is more controllable. I know exactly how each scan performs. Actually, there is no such thing as true randomness in anything that is manufactured, unless it is taken from nature, which has a periodicity that goes into eons. Algorithms can be used to generate pseudorandom numbers."

Ricketts paused. He was about to touch on one of the most important elements of the box, one that goes into not only mathematics but also metaphysical territory.

"The random scans I use come from a random numbers generator program that I wrote, which is also part of the imbedded process capability in the microprocessor. It depends on a seed number. Transcendental, one-way mathematical functions provide results which are random in nature over hundreds of millions of iterations, but which eventually repeat. When the MiniBox Plus is turned on, it is born with the seed number of three seventy-seven, a combination of very powerful numbers, three and seven. Every time the scan is changed, a snapshot is taken of a counter that is always running inside the computer. It gets chopped down, and that becomes the new seed number the next time the machine is started. When you turn it on, the jumps and hops in the scan will not be anything like the last time you turned it on. Thus, I actually do have true randomness built into the box. That's something only a mathematician would appreciate but to me is important to my philosophy about using the vibrational energy of numbers."

In the mystery traditions, numbers are not quantities. They are ideas or forms that constitute the building blocks of all things in the universe. Each number has it own vibration, character, and attributes, which in turn influence the physical world by attracting certain energies. The vibrational importance of numbers has been recognized since ancient times.

The number three plays a prominent role in myth, mysticism, folklore, alchemy, and the dynamics of spiritual change. Three opens the gateways to the higher planes—it symbolizes creation and ascent. It is concerned with fate, destiny, and synchronicity. When things happen in threes, one should pay attention, for the universe is sending a wake-up call.

Seven is a universal sacred number of the macrocosm and divinity. It is the number of mystical man, the sum of three (spirit) and four (the material), thus making the perfect order. It embodies the search for wisdom, discovery, the hero's quest for spiritual truth, and investigation, research, and analysis. It is concerned with the growth of spirit, philosophy, the need to rely upon intuition, and the need to meditate on what has been learned. It is the number of rest (God rested on the seventh day of creation) and spiritual realization. It is associated with magical, psychic, and healing powers.

From the standpoint of metaphysical philosophy, then, 377 brings powerful spiritual forces into the programming and operation of the box. We have forces in motion of logic, intuition, the psychic, and the spiritual. Many scientists would shudder at such a connection involving numbers, but we believe that the day will soon come when science and the metaphysical and mystical will merge to create a new disciplinary understanding of the cosmos. Perhaps the ghost boxes will play a significant role!

Let's return to the Slaughters' dining room in Texas. They turned on the MiniBox Plus. Within a minute, voices were speaking in German, quite an oddity for the Dallas–Fort Worth area. The experiences of European EVP researchers in the past have shown that communicators often speak in different languages, sometimes multiple ones in the same session. They even switch languages in mid-sentence. Interestingly, the languages are always known to at least one person present. The Slaughters and Rosemary do not speak German—but Ricketts does.

Rosemary was intrigued because she did have a German connection regarding the box. She had been researching the work of Franz Seidl, an earlier Austrian researcher in real-time Electronic Voice Phenomena, and had obtained one of his books, written in German. Her research colleague, the well-known ufologist and Earth mysteries expert Philip J. Imbrogno, was translating it for her. "Do you know Franz Seidl?" she asked the communicators. "Phil Imbrogno is translating some of his work for me."

A female voice came through in English: "Thank him."

We learned at press time that, due to personal reasons, Ron Ricketts has retired from making MiniBoxes. His work has inspired others to follow in his footsteps.

BEYOND THE BOXES

As intriguing as radio scan devices are, they have limitations. Holding a connection is one of them. Every sweep of the radio band is different. Some researchers see too many hazards in misinterpretation of stray words.

Another way of generating real-time Electronic Voice Phenomena uses small bits of human speech: fragments of words called phonemes and allophones. A phoneme is the smallest unit of sound, such as the "g" sound in "gather." The term "phoneme" is derived from the Greek word *phōnēma,* which means "a sound uttered." Allophones are variants of phonemes. For example, an allophone determines whether a "g" sound is harsh or soft. Some devices and software programs use these fragments as streams of sound from which whole words, phrases, and sentences are produced. The idea behind them is that the possibility of misidentification and contamination from broadcast sources can be greatly reduced or eliminated. Phonemes tend to be clearer and more humanlike in sounds, while allophones sound robotic and produce more stuttering and chatter.

EVPmaker, developed by Stefan Bion of Germany, is an experimental software that uses speech fragments to generate acoustic "raw material." Experimenters record speech, and the program chops the words into fragments and plays them back continuously in random order. The result sounds like gibberish, but meaningful communications pop out in Electronic Voice Phenomena, both recorded and real-time.

Bill Chappell, an electrical engineer in Colorado, created the Ovilus, a handheld device that takes EMF (electromagnetic frequency) readings and turns them into words from a programmed internal dictionary. It also has a phonetic generator and several modes of operation. A video Ovilus features goggles and an infrared camera. Another device of Chappell's is the Paranormal Puck. It works on a computer and also turns environmental data (EMF and temperature) into words that appear on the screen or can be heard. A version uses phonemes. The Puck also captures images.

Chappell was working on creating digital dowsing rods and new types of EMF equipment when someone approached him about getting into high-tech spirit communications. "I thought it was a joke," he told us. "It wasn't until after I built the first piece of equipment and had a pretty significant run-in with it that I thought maybe something else was occurring." His devices made their appearances on the market in 2008 and continue in ever new and experimental models often used in paranormal investigation.

One of his simplest and first creations is the most popular: a modified, inexpensive Radio Shack AM radio known as the "Shack hack." A simple clip or bend of a wire on the circuit board turns a regular radio into one with a linear sweep, making it an inexpensive version of a ghost box.

While these devices are a decade or less old, they owe their existence to more than a century of technological development and the genius of inventors such as Thomas Alva Edison, Nikola Tesla, Guglielmo Marconi, Alexander Graham Bell, and Samuel F. B. Morse. The titans of telecommunications, energy, and industry did more than unite human beings—they touched infinity.

3

High Tech in the Séance Room

The first time I heard Electronic Voice Phenomena was as a listener to my predecessor, Art Bell, when he was hosting *Coast to Coast AM*. At the time I had my own show in St. Louis, *Night Talk with the Night Hawk*. On this particular night, Art was interviewing some ghost investigators and he played EVP clips that they had captured. The voices sounded odd and were faint and fleeting, hard to catch, but it was obvious to me that they were voices talking, giving meaningful answers to questions that had been asked. It was riveting to think that we might indeed be getting voice messages directly from people who had died. I knew I had to find out more about Electronic Voice

Phenomena, how it was done, and who was doing the research.

Although every era has its "tech," our current spirit communications technology has its roots in the nineteenth-century séance room. Before the age of telecommunications, one of the centers of the spirit universe was not an exotic cosmic address but a primitive log cabin in Athens County, Ohio. In the 1850s, this quiet rural farmland was jarred into multidimensional reality by a theater of spirits, who communicated in ear-shattering intensity via musical instruments and innovative technology. People made pilgrimages from all over the world to see it in action. They did not go home disappointed.

The "Spirit Room" log cabin belonged to Jonathan Koons, an unlikely soul to usher in the era of technology to spirit communications. He was neither a scientist nor an inventor but a simple, self-educated farming man. He was well-read in philosophy, news, and politics, however, and he possessed the right kind of curious mind. Koons innocently opened the door to the spirit world, and spirits flooded in to talk to the living. Spirit communications would never be the same again. The age of machines to contact the dead had arrived.

Mediumship has been a tried-and-true way of contacting the spirit world since ancient times. The messages are filtered through a person. Koons and others like him wanted something more: direct spirit communication without a middle person doing the talking. The spirits even gave instructions how to make the devices that would enable direct communication to take place.

CALLING ALL SPIRITS

Koons's interest was ignited by the Spiritualism movement, which officially began in America in 1848, sparked by a media sensation known as the Fox sisters. The Fox family, who lived in Hydesville, New York, believed their house to be haunted. Two of the young Fox daughters, Maggie and Katie, discovered that they could communicate with the alleged ghost with rapping sounds. By asking questions, then asking for raps by letter of the alphabet, the girls could get messages. It was both tedious and thrilling. Soon the neighbors were entranced, and then the story hit the newspapers. Maggie and Katie Fox became instant celebrities. Huge audiences wanted to see them perform. They began touring and giving public programs, managed by their older sister, Leah.

The Fox sisters did not create a movement but merely lit the match to the tinderbox. For some time, the public had been increasingly primed to seek communication with the spirit world, thanks in part to the fascination with mesmerism. Named after the French doctor Franz Anton Mesmer, who practiced from the mid–eighteenth century to the early nineteenth century, "mesmerism" was the early term for hypnotism. Mesmer had discovered that putting people into trances aided the healing of certain ailments.

There were some unexpected and surprising side effects: some mesmerized subjects, called "sonambules," were suddenly psychic and mediumistic and could communicate with spirits through automatic writing or voice mediumship. It wasn't long before the commercial side of this was seized upon and traveling mesmerists took to the stage to entertain audiences with entranced subjects who could talk to the dead.

The Fox sisters never envisioned themselves as performers or prophets, but they were carried along by public demand. People wanted to talk to spirits and were willing to pay for the privilege. Some of the audience wanted proof of the afterlife, and this newest twist on mediumship held out tantalizing promise.

As the Spiritualism fad burgeoned, countless individuals "discovered" their own mediumistic gifts. Some were undoubtedly genuine, and some were undoubtedly driven by the prospects of fame and fortune. Fame—mostly fleeting—came to many, but fortune eluded them all. Talking to spirits has never been a way to get rich, then or now.

In 1852 Koons read a newspaper account about them. Intrigued, he decided to investigate this phenomenon. He attended several séances held by freshly minted mediums in Ohio. At one of them, the spirits told him via a medium that he, too, possessed "the gift." In fact, he was told, he was "the most powerful medium on earth." What was more, his wife, Abigail, and all of his nine children, including a seven-month-old infant, also possessed "the gift."

Excited, Koons returned home to announce this news. The family began holding private séances. The spirits were quite chatty. Soon the spirits were issuing instructions for improving communications. The Koonses were to build a "Spirit Room." The spirits were insistent that their instructions be followed to the letter, including the dimensions of the room and its furnishings and equipment.

SPIRIT SPECTACLES IN A NEWFANGLED ERA

Koons started construction immediately. The "room" was actually a self-contained log cabin used only for spirit communications. It measured twelve by fourteen feet and had three windows covered with shutters. The furniture consisted of benches that held about twenty to thirty people in a circle. The equipment included a tenor drum, bass drum, two fiddles, a guitar, an accordion, a trumpet, a tin horn, a tea bell, triangle, and a tambourine. There also were two tables at the center of the circle, a rack for the instruments, wire for suspending bells, and doves cut from copper sheets.

In addition—and this was the key to the high tech of the times—Koons was told by the spirits to build a "spirit machine," a device that was a complex arrangement of copper and zinc tubing. The spirit machine would collect and focus the "magnetic aura" in the room, which would help the spirits manifest and communicate. The device was in effect an electromagnetic battery.

Finding all this stuff in rural Ohio was not an easy

task, and Koons was a man of modest means. Driven by his newfound zeal, however, Koons managed to beg and borrow money and instruments. Soon his Spirit Room was ready for action.

The show was spectacular, especially for rural Ohio. After the spectators were seated on the benches, Jonathan and Abigail and their eldest son, Nahum, eighteen, took seats at the tables. The lights were put out, and Jonathan played his fiddle. The "spirit machine" did its job focusing the magnetic aura. Within minutes, Koons was joined by a cacophony of music played on the other instruments by invisible spirits. The spirits did not just make racket but played tunes, albeit unknown ones. Witnesses reported that the instruments flew and danced through the air. The noise was deafening and could be heard for up to a mile away.

The spirits also sang along to their music in an unknown language, their "unearthly" voices sending chills through the amazed witnesses.

There was still more to the show. A central spirit spoke through the tin horn, which, like a megaphone, amplified the voice. The spirit introduced himself as John King and said that in his last life he had been a Welsh pirate named Henry Morgan in the seventeenth century. He seemed quite exotic and dashing to the simple farming folk of the Midwest. King served as a disembodied ringmaster, marshaling a band of 165 spirits called "Oress." The Oress said they had once been part of a race of humans called "Adam" that had existed thousands of years before the biblical Adam. John King was the foremost among them. Their leaders were ancient angels.

After the music and the charm of John King came spirit hands, ghostly manifestations of disembodied hands that touched some of the witnesses. The hands were described as clammy and cold, and one doctor likened them to the doughy hands of corpses he autopsied. How on earth or in heaven did solid hands manifest from the spirit world?

Charles Partridge, a writer who attended one of the Koonses' séances in 1855, reported that the audience heard a chorus of disembodied voices "singing in our room most exquisitely. I think I never heard such perfect harmony. Spirit hands and arms were formed in our presence several times, and by aid of a solution of phosphorous, prepared at their request by Mr. Koons, they were seen as distinctly as in a light room."

No wonder the Koonses' Spirit Room absolutely rocked Ohio! Word spread like wildfire, and people trekked in from considerable distances for a chance to sit on a bench. The farm was located in a remote area in the shadow of Mount Nebo, near the border between Ohio and what was then Virginia (now West Virginia), and was difficult to reach. The last two miles had to be undertaken on foot. Nonetheless, the pilgrims poured in. Many were put up for the night. The Koons home was packed with people coming and going at all times. The family never charged a penny for the séances, but many of the pilgrims made modest donations, usually barely enough to cover the Koonses' expenses.

Meanwhile, jealous neighbors eyed the Spirit Room popularity and thought a financial bonanza was in the making. They decided to cash in, too. The Tippie family, which included husband and wife and ten children, lived on another remote farm in the Ohio countryside, about two to three miles from the Koons farm. Suddenly the entire Tippie family were mediums. The Tippies copied the Koonses' Spirit Room and duplicated all their spirit voices and manifestations. They even copied the copper and zinc "spirit machine" for focusing the "magnetic aura." The Tippies drew an eager audience but never eclipsed the Koonses in show. Perhaps the Tippies just didn't have the right mojo and were not as mediumistic as they claimed to be. More than a century on, spirit communications researchers would learn over and over again that the human mediumistic factor weighs heavily on success with devices and machines for reaching into the Beyond.

The Koonses certainly made no riches off the spirits, and it is doubtful that the Tippies did, either. The Koonses' Spirit Room operated until 1858, when the family abandoned their spirit activity, abruptly packed up and moved to Illinois, and became wandering missionaries with messages from the Beyond. In actuality, they fell into a publicity black hole, never to make the Spiritualist scene again.

What happened to them was to become a familiar problem for others trying to bridge the interdimensional void, on down into current times. The Koonses were harassed, threatened, and attacked by religious zealots who said they had no business poking into God's business: if God wanted people to talk to the dead, he would arrange it himself. During the six years that the Koonses ran their Spirit Room, they were repeatedly attacked by angry mobs who burned down their barns and set fire to their crops and even beat their children.

EARLY SPIRIT TECH

In those heady days of séances, spirit communication was two-way and real-time but still had a long way to go in terms of technology. The Koonses' "spirit machine" died with the ending of their activities, but the use of tech caught hold. Some mediums became "direct voice" mouthpieces. Instead of using the medium's vocal cords, the spirits spoke directly out of the air, aided somehow by the medium's trance. Direct spirit voices were often thin and whispery and were hard to understand. A new tool to amplify direct spirit voices then made more frequent séance appearances: the trumpet.

Séance trumpets were not the same as musical trumpets. They were more like megaphones, usually made out of tin or aluminum. Some were made out of cardboard. Participants at a séance could hear whispery spirit voices better by placing the small end of a megaphone at their ear. The medium would hold a palm over the broad end. Supposedly the spirits would then speak into the broad end and the sound would be amplified at the ear. Sometimes the small end of the trumpet was placed directly on a medium's larynx. One immediately thinks that ventriloquism could have been used to produce spirit voices, but often the voices sounded from distant corners of the séance room, not directly near the medium.

Trumpets were a handy tool. They could be brought out when a medium's voice failed—or simply for the staging of mediumistic pyrotechnics. There were many dazzling displays of séance trumpets. They were said to float in the air around the participants. Sometimes visible ghostly spirit hands would manipulate them, as they did with the instruments in the Koonses' Spirit Room.

ECTOPLASMIC MATERIALIZATIONS

One other early phenomenon of importance was ectoplasm, for it would play a role later on in modern spirit communications. Ectoplasm was a white or gray substance that oozed out of the bodies of mediums and took on shapes of alleged spirits in the forms of hands, faces, and even entire apparitional bodies. Sometimes it was just long and stringy. Ectoplasmic materializations were quite a crowd pleaser in séances but also were highly controversial—and sometimes done fraudulently.

Ectoplasm may have been known as early as the seventeenth century. The term "ectoplasm" was coined in 1894 by Charles Richet, a French physiologist who was studying the Italian medium Eusapia Palladino. At one séance,

Richet and another sitter were holding tight to the medium's hands to prevent fraud. Behind a curtain, a lump began protruding into the room. Richet grabbed it and was astonished to feel a large, rubbery hand with sausage-like fingers that ended at the wrist. Richet combined two Greek words, *ektos* and *plasma*, to mean "exteriorized substance." He was mystified by it and said that it was "absurd but absolutely true."

Ectoplasm was described variously as cold, rubberlike, warm, textured, doughlike, cordlike, gelatinous, warm, sticky, light, and vaporous. It was also often described as smelly and sometimes as having an odor like ozone. Blobs and strings of it came out of mediums' noses, ears, mouths, navels, and other body parts. When the séance was over the ectoplasm snapped back into the medium's body or withered or disintegrated. Mediums said they could not explain materialization but shrugged and said it was up to science to find out the laws pertaining to it. Scientists were baffled.

TECH TAKES OFF

By the 1930s, scientists who studied mediums were still coming up empty-handed for hard proof of survival and the afterlife and the public was jaded with the shows. Physical mediumship has never disappeared, however; in fact, in recent years it has enjoyed a revival along with the overall interest in high-tech spirit communications. Ectoplasm and materializations are still on the scene.

Meanwhile, interest in contact with spirits mutated into other forms of exploration. Phenomenal power could be harnessed, and high-tech communications promised to revolutionize life on earth and turn the world into a global community. The dead would not be left out—they would see to that.

4

The Strange Signals of Morse, Marconi, and Tesla

In 1838 Samuel F. B. Morse, the namesake of Morse code, made history by sending a long-distance telegraph message using electromagnetism and wire. The message, encoded in clicks, traveled across forty-five miles of wire stretched between Baltimore and Washington, D.C. It said: "What hath God wrought?" That prophetic question echoed on down through the decades as each new communication invention not only linked the living but opened the door to the spirit world and other dimensions as well. The dead, it seems, have been very fast to seize whatever we invent as a way to talk to us.

There was no voice transmission in telegraphy, of course, but that didn't stop mystery communicators from tap-tap-tapping away. Researchers received odd messages from unknown communicators and even from people known to be dead. These messages were often dismissed as curiosities.

The big breakthrough in communications came with the discovery of radio waves. Awestruck researchers found that outer space is not silent but alive with sound. Everything in the cosmos emits its own frequency of radio waves, which are a form of electromagnetic radiation. The universe sings away in a cacophony of radio wave voices— hisses, roars, whistles, groans, and moans. The sun talks, the planets and stars talk, the Earth talks, and everything on the Earth talks—even the rocks. All of these frequencies, we have learned, are potential background carriers for interdimensional communication.

Radio waves were predicted mathematically in 1864 by James Clerk Maxwell, a Scottish mathematician and theoretical physicist, but it was not until 1888 that a German physicist named Heinrich Hertz confirmed the existence of them by actually producing them in his laboratory. He did so with a spark discharge of an induction coil. Hertz measured wavelengths and their velocities and rates of oscillation. These waves were initially called "Hertzian waves" or "aetheric waves." Today we know them as radio waves, which are measured in units called hertz.

Radio waves take up only a portion of the electromagnetic spectrum. Radio waves are longer than light waves and range from 0.5 centimeters to 30,000 meters in length. The waves oscillate in cycles; one hertz is one cycle per second. The range of radio wave oscillation is from three hertz to one gigahertz. "Giga" is a "prefix multiplier" used in electronics and physics. You are probably familiar with prefix multipliers in terms of storage on your computer: kilobytes, megabytes, gigabytes, and so on. A "giga" denotes 10^9, or a multiplier of 1 billion. "Kilo" is one thousand, and "mega" is 1 million. So, you can see how amazingly big just the radio portion of the electromagnetic spectrum is, from three cycles per second to 1 billion cycles. The human ear hears only a tiny portion of that, from about 12Hz to 20KHz. With technology, we can extend our range of hearing into further reaches of the entire electromagnetic spectrum. Spirit communications researchers today constantly search for the best frequency for tuning in the dead.

In its infancy, radio was called "wireless" or "wireless telegraphy," because the transmission of waves was accomplished without wires.

Many people credit the Italian inventor Guglielmo Marconi with the development of radio broadcast, but in fact the credit goes to Nikola Tesla, a Serb who immigrated to America in 1884 and went to work for Thomas Edison. Marconi became interested in the applications of electricity and began experimenting with ways to transmit messages without wires, first with short waves.

In 1895 Marconi succeeded in sending radio signals over a distance of 1.5 miles. In 1896 he took his device to

England, where he felt he would be able to do better research. In 1897 he sent a signal over twelve miles, and in 1899 he transmitted across the English Channel between England and France. In 1901 he transmitted across the Atlantic, from Cornwall, England to Newfoundland, Canada.

Marconi at first transmitted Morse code, not voice, over radio. The first radio voice transmission was made on December 23, 1900, by Prof. Reginald Aubrey Fessenden in Maryland.

Marconi continued his research, which eventually led to microwave radiotelephone connections. In 1909 he shared the Nobel Prize with Prof. Karl Ferdinand Braun for their advancements in wireless telegraphy.

Tesla found Hertz's induction coil to be impractical. He developed what became known as the Tesla coil, a series of high-frequency alternators that could produce up to 33KHz. In 1893 he described a system for wireless telegraphy, and in 1898 he was awarded a patent on wireless transmission, two years before Marconi filed for his original patent.

Tesla, who never got the fame and recognition he deserved, sued Marconi in 1915 for infringing on his patent. Marconi denied that he had ever read any of Tesla's material—but he lost the lawsuit.

UNKNOWN COMMUNICATORS

Despite the controversy over who was first, Marconi, Tesla, and others heard unknown signals. For years, Tesla had predicted that communications with Mars and other planets was imminent. Intelligent Martians were a "statistical certainty," he claimed, and human beings had everything to gain by establishing communication with them. Ever hopeful and utopian in his vision for the future of humanity, Tesla believed that interplanetary contact would lift earthlings into a spiritual light.

"I think that nothing can be more important than interplanetary communication," Tesla asserted. "It will certainly come someday and the certitude that there are other human beings in the universe, working, suffering, struggling, like ourselves, will produce a magic effect on mankind and will build the foundation of a universal brotherhood that will last as long as humanity itself."

Few of his fellow human beings shared his cosmic perception. The idea of communicating with aliens was, well, *alien* to a world that had yet to transition to the automobile. One reporter, writing in *The Pittsburgh Dispatch* on February 23, 1901, criticized Tesla: "Some of his sanguine conceptions, including the transmission of signals to Mars, have evoked the opinion that it would be better for Mr. Tesla to predict less and do more in the line of performance." The reporter did not state whose opinion he was evoking—perhaps it was his own.

Tesla, however, was far ahead of everyone's game. He was not only a brilliant inventor; he was a visionary in the truest sense of the word and a mystic as well. He saw a different reality than most people. He described how, as early as age three, he saw auras and sparks of light around everything. People were lit with halos of light, footprints were illumined with glows, and stroking the fur of his pet cat set off showers of sparky lights. His brain hummed along day and night, pushing back ordinary reality to allow inspiration from some infinite source to pour in. The failure of mortals to understand his genius was of trifling importance to him. He was consumed with ideas, a cosmic brain always on fire but trapped in a human body.

Tesla was not only convinced of extraterrestrial contact; he was also convinced that aliens were already on the planet, hidden from view. In 1899 he told a reporter, "We cannot even with positive assurance assert that some of them [otherworldly beings] might not be present here in this world, in the very midst of us . . . their life manifestations may be such that we are unable to see them."

It was an astonishing statement for a time when few people entertained the idea of life beyond Earth, much less thought of actual contact in any way. Tesla's idea of aliens being on Earth but beyond our senses forecast later ideas in physics of parallel dimensions. Perhaps parallel dimensions are the originating points of unknown voices, as many modern spirit communications researchers now believe. Tesla, in his brilliance, was a century ahead of the curve.

DID TESLA HAVE CONTACT?

Tesla's first inkling of actual interplanetary contact came in 1900, the same year that Fessenden was working on the first terrestrial-based radio voice broadcast. At the time, Tesla was in his laboratory near Colorado Springs, where he had built a powerful radio receiver. He was working on a device that could pick up approaching storms, so sensitive that it would register electrical changes eleven hundred miles away.

One night he became aware of rhythmic sounds coming over the receiver. He was both puzzled and awestruck and at first had no idea what they were. Later he surmised that they were coming from an intelligent source and figured that Mars or Venus would be the most likely place.

Writing in *Collier's Weekly* in 1901, Tesla poured on his typical drama:

> I can never forget the first sensations I experienced when it dawned upon me that I had observed something possibly of incalculable consequences to mankind. I felt as though I were present at the birth of a new knowledge or the revelation of a great truth. My first observations positively terrified me as there was present in them something mysterious, not to say supernatural, and I was alone at my laboratory at night; but at the time the idea of these disturbances being intelligently controlled signals did not yet present itself to me.

Tesla went on to say that he was familiar with the electrical disturbances of the sun, the aurora borealis, and Earth currents and could confidently rule all of them out.

Nor were the signals the product of atmospheric disturbances.

"It was sometime afterward when the thought flashed upon my mind that the disturbances I had observed might be due to an intelligent control," he said. "Although I could not at the time decipher their meaning, it was impossible for me to think of them as having been entirely accidental. The feeling is constantly growing on me that I had been the first to hear the greeting of one planet to another. A purpose was behind these electrical signals."

Decades on, radio astronomers said that Tesla probably was picking up stellar radio waves. Maybe so, but perhaps he was hearing some form of interdimensional communication, perhaps from nonhuman beings, as he thought, or perhaps from the human dead. Tesla's awe was significant and similar to the awe expressed by today's spirit communications researchers who hear live unknown voices for the first time.

Tesla's ideas about interplanetary communication were picked up by a few of his peers. Marconi heard strange signals, too, and wondered about them being nonhuman in origin. Yet he was dismissed by others as having mistaken stray radio signals from distant places on Earth. Signals coming from off the planet were too much for most people of Marconi's and Tesla's day.

In January 1919, Marconi told a reporter for the *Daily Chronicle* in London that he had often received signals "out of the ether" that seemed to come from beyond the Earth, possibly the stars. "Communication with intelligence on other stars . . . may some day be possible, and as many of the planets are much older than ours the beings who live there ought to have information for us of enormous value," he said.

When the reporter objected that language might be a barrier, Marconi acknowledged that it might be an obstacle but was not insurmountable. Mathematics, he said, might be the common tongue.

A year later, the press reported on Marconi's investigations into the sources of the strange signals. The French media had for the most part written them off as a joke, with such headlines as "Hello, Central, Give Me the Moon." The press in England and America took the matter more seriously. Calling them "very queer sounds and indications," Marconi said the signals mimicked Morse code but could not be translated into anything intelligible. They were received simultaneously in London and New York, indicating that they were coming from vast distances. Echoing Tesla, Marconi opined that the signals possibly could be intelligent signals coming from Mars or some other off-planet source.

French radio experts still disparaged Marconi's ideas, claiming that no such signals had been received at the radio receiver on the Eiffel Tower. Surely if aliens were communicating with Earth, they would be contacting the French! "Frankly, I am in ignorance of this supernatural correspondence," sniffed M. Baillaud, the director of the Paris Observatory.

Tesla persisted in promoting the idea of using technology

to reach out beyond the Earth. In so doing, he anticipated both the coming age of radio astronomy and the age of high-tech spirit communications. Science would follow the path of radio astronomy, looking for intelligent signals from the far reaches of space.

Years later, EVP researchers found that not all of their communicators said they were dead—some said they were alien beings from other planets and worlds.

Let's move on to one of the big controversies that continue to this day: what did Thomas Edison know about communicating with the dead, and did he ever invent a telephone or other device that could do it?

5

The Mystery of Edison's Telephone
to the Spirit World

Thomas Alva Edison, one of the world's greatest inventors, played a key role in our electricity and telecommunications systems. With more than one thousand patents to his name, Edison earned the title of The Wizard of Menlo Park, after the location of his laboratories in Menlo Park, New Jersey.

Much has been written about Edison, both favorable and unfavorable. He has been described as a genius and great thinker and criticized as an opportunist who took other people's ideas to the bank via the patent office. He was a shrewd and calculating businessman, and more than once he blocked Tesla, his onetime employee, from getting ahead of him. It is evident from Edison's interviews that his mind was always turning with creativity. While Tesla had his visionary head out in the stars, Edison had his practical head oriented to the world of commerce and profits. Genius, he was fond of saying, is 1 percent inspiration and 99 percent perspiration.

Edison gave a lot of thought to the continuation of life after death. For him, mesmerism, spiritualism, and electricity combined into a strange and fertile brew, offering intriguing ideas about the material versus the immaterial. Death brought an end to the material body, but an immaterial part of a human being, perhaps the mind and/or spirit, seemed to have the capability of taking on materiality, such as in voice communications.

It is hard to know just exactly how Edison felt about *communication* between the living and the dead, for he made contradictory statements. He was not an atheist, as some said, for he believed in a supreme intelligence. He was not fond of organized religion. On one hand, he seemed intrigued enough by the idea of communication with the dead. On the other hand, he rejected the idea of spirits and their ability to manifest in accordance with Spiritualist views. The brain was like a machine in his view, and science would explain everything, including a way to communicate with the dead—if such a thing existed.

Edison may have started thinking about using a telephone to dial up the dead as soon as Alexander Graham Bell made the first completed call in 1876. Ever since Edison died in 1931, a story has circulated that he had attempted to invent such a telephone or device. That story is still widely believed today. There is no hard evidence to back it up, however—no machine, no documentation. We have some tantalizing statements made on record by Edison but little else.

EDISON ADDRESSES THE AFTERLIFE

By the 1920s, both radio and telephones were making their way to the masses. Edison was not the only researcher who thought that both offered intriguing possibilities for reaching out to the dead. He spent most of his life as an agnostic, but he evidently started thinking more about the hereafter in the last decade or so of his life. *Why couldn't the dead and the living communicate?* he wondered. Perhaps a telephonic device could be built.

We know that he at least thought about it even if he did not actually work on it, for he did make statements pertaining to talking to the dead. On December 26, 1920, he was quoted in *Le Soir*, a Brussels newspaper, as saying that he did not know if the personality survives death, but he wished to build an apparatus that would "give the spirits an opportunity to communicate more efficiently than the tilt top tables, the blows [rapping and knocking], the ouija board and other rough methods." Evidently Edison was disdainful of some of the common but earnest ways that people were using in their attempts to talk to spirits.

Edison also said he had no interest in "conversing with Cleopatra's or Napoleon's shadow" but wanted to help "superior entities" who were familiar with electricity demonstrate the survival of their ego. He said that drawings that had been published of him communicating with the dead through a type of wireless radio were "absurd."

On January 23, 1921, journalist A. D. Rothman wrote an intriguing article on Edison published in *The New York Times*. It was headlined "Mr. Edison's 'Life Units,'" with the subhead "Hundred Trillion in Human Body May Scatter After Death—Machine to Register Them." Rothman's article began: "Without a peer in the field of scientific invention, Thomas Edison has announced his entrance into a new sphere, that of psychic research." Rothman noted that Edison's intentions were "greatly misunderstood" by many and that scientists and clerics had both advised him "not trespass on lands not his own." Nonetheless, the inventor felt that he might contribute to knowledge of the afterlife, thus providing comfort to the millions of grieving persons who had lost loved ones in the world war.

Edison stressed in his interview with Rothman that he was approaching the afterlife as a scientist, not as a spiritist. "I do not know what the word 'spiritual' means," he said. "I am not interested in matter of spirit. I am conducting a laboratory experiment." Rothman wrote:

> He was even very reluctant to discuss the machine he was reported to be building for the apprehension of messages from the dead. He did admit that he was engaged—he had been engaged for a num-

ber of years—in the construction of such an apparatus. He even indicated the principle on which he felt it would work, namely: upon the principle of control, whereby a man with one-eighth of a horsepower is able to set into motion machinery with hundreds of thousands of horsepower. Beyond that, however, he was not prepared at the present time to speak. . . . What the public is interested in, Mr. Edison pointed out, is results only, and that was what he was striving for.

Edison went on to expound on his theories on life, death, and the afterlife. Everything boiled down to "physico-chemical reactions." Rather than having individual souls, human beings might be part of one great soul that is the sum of everything in existence, he said. The body and personality were composed of up to 100 trillion infinitely small packets of energy that Edison called "life units." The life units did not perish upon death but continued on, perhaps separating and scattering. When a physical body wore out due to illness or old age, the body died and the life units swarmed to enter a new body. The number of life units is fixed, Edison said, and so "it is the same entities that have served over and over again."

Pressed by Rothman, Edison was vague on where he thought the life units went immediately after death. Perhaps they went into a new body, he speculated, saying, "I have no information on the subject." Pressed again, this time for details on how such a machine could be built and how it would work, Edison was again evasive. "What difference does it make?" he told Rothman. "There are half a dozen ways of making the machine or approaching the problem." He declined to give a specific description of the machine. He repeated that such a device would use very little power to put into motion a vague "far greater power."

Evidently the machine was not built at the time of the interview, for Rothman said that Edison "hopes to build" a machine that would register the life units.

> He is not prepared to say if he succeeds in constructing an apparatus that can register the stimuli of personality units . . . that it will mean the opening of free communication with the dead. What Mr. Edison does say is that if his theories should prove correct and should his apparatus succeed in apprehending the stimuli, it will be the first step in a correct understanding of the entire problem of life and death, and will lead the way to concrete development of communication with the dead.

Rothman asked him if he believed that communication with the dead was indeed possible. Edison replied, "There is a doubt. I am not sure. That's the reason I am experimenting. But if I didn't believe, I wouldn't try."

Later in 1921, Edison again commented on the spirit world, in an article he wrote himself for *Scientific American*:

If our personality survives, then it is strictly logical or scientific to assume that it retains memory, intellect, other faculties and knowledge that we acquire on this Earth. Therefore, if personality exists after what we call death, it is reasonable to conclude that those who leave the Earth would like to communicate with those they have left here. I am inclined to believe that our personality hereafter will be able to affect matter. If this reasoning be correct, then, if we can evolve an instrument so delicate as to be affected by our personality as it survives in the next life, such an instrument, when made available, ought to record something.

In 1926, Edison wrote in *The People* that his research supported life after death, and he was inclined to think that communication was possible.

Was Edison serious? Some believe today that he was just pulling a big joke about the afterlife and communication with the dead. If he did work on an actual device, what was it? Many believe that it was a telephone-like apparatus that would link the living and the dead. However, in the interviews just cited Edison spoke of a different kind of device, one that would register the life units, which in turn would pave the way for communications.

If Edison actually started work on any kind of spirit device, he apparently left no prototype or plans behind when he died. We could not find it or any papers related to it, nor has anyone else ever produced convincing documentation of it. Still, reports have persisted—almost like urban folklore—that a prototype was built and others saw it. If Edison had a specific plan in mind, he left no concrete clues behind him. It was his habit to be very secretive about his inventions until he patented them. Nonetheless, no notes, diaries, or models have ever been found among his records. The controversy over his words and intention continues.

In 1941 an alleged blueprint of Edison's device was "found" in New York. The device was said to have consisted of a microphone in a wooden box with a large aluminum trumpet filled with potassium permanganate and crossed by an electrode. A wire connected the microphone to the trumpet and an antenna.

Potassium permanganate is a water-soluble salt of purple-black crystals that oxidizes easily and today has mostly medicinal uses. It is highly volatile. In an aluminum trumpet, it would have heated up and acted as an electrolyte. Supposedly this device would amplify "ether waves" carrying spirit voices. Operating models were built from this blueprint but failed to work. The blueprint is widely considered to be a hoax and not the actual work of Edison.

Edison may not have actually built a prototypical communications device, but he may have tried to document evidence of the afterlife. In October 1933, *Modern Mechanix and Inventions* magazine published an anonymously written article, "Edison's Own Secret," about an alleged failed experiment he conducted in 1920. The experiment was rather primitive. He set up a photoelectric cell and a lamp that gave off a pencil-thin beam of light. The beam struck the surface of the cell and was transformed into a weak electric current. Anything that cut the beam would register on the cell's meter. Edison had Spiritualists invoke the dead and ask them to walk through the beam of light. According to the article, an unspecified number of hours passed, but nothing registered on the meter.

The article also said that Edison kept quiet about the experiment because of its failure. How everyone else managed to do so remains a mystery; the article gives no names for the other scientists and the Spiritualists who allegedly took part. Another mystery is why the article was written thirteen years later—and two years after Edison had died and could not refute nor verify the event.

OTHERWORLDLY TELEPHONES

Edison was by no means the only inventor wondering about a telephonic device to the dead. Long before he spoke up on the subject, others were trying to adapt the telephone to spirit communications. One in the late nineteenth century was a "telephonic apparatus" developed by J. B. McIndoe of Glasgow, Scotland. The apparatus was a sensitive telephone transmitter that, like a trumpet, was placed directly on a medium's larynx. Sitters at a séance were connected to the transmitter with a telephone receiver through which they could hear the spirit voices. Such feats were more impressive when done under daylight conditions, so that sitters could see everything done by the medium. The medium, however, remained the main instrument delivering the spirit communications. The telephonic device was more like a glorified trumpet, providing amplification.

In 1921, the same year that Edison was expounding his vague ideas in the press, a psychical researcher in Nottingham, England, F. R. Melton, announced that he had invented a "psychic telephone." Melton said he received voices of the dead through his machine, and he published details about the machine's construction and operation. The device itself seemed incredibly simple: a telephone apparatus hooked to an amplifier and placed inside a small box. The apparatus was a twenty-three-inch-long trumpet-shaped aluminum tube that was three inches in diameter at one end and eight inches in diameter at the other. One end had a receiver and the other an amplifier. The voices were heard over a telephone-like headset.

Melton had gotten the idea for his psychic telephone from his son, George, who had served as a Morse code operator during the world war. George had often gotten unidentified transmissions, and wondered if they were coming from the freshly killed on the battlefields.

The Meltons' interests took a serious turn after the war was over. In 1920 media reports circulated of wireless operators receiving mysterious messages. Some thought they were coming from outer space, but the Meltons were inclined to believe the dead were the source. By this time, George had discovered that he was mediumistic. He attended a séance, at which he fell into a trance and an entity who identified himself as W.G. said he would help George design a "spirit telephone" that would help people develop their psychic abilities.

F.R. built his psychic telephone with the intention that anyone could use it successfully, but the first version of it tended to work only when George was present. This may be one of the first indicators that machines and devices intended for interdimensional communication seem to function better when—and sometimes only when—operated by people who have psychic or mediumistic gifts.

F.R. redesigned his device hoping to get around the mediumistic obstacle, but without much success. He eliminated the original aluminum tube. He added a balloon, which was blown up by a medium. The mediumistic breath created a "psychic ether" that would amplify spirit voices, he said. The balloon was placed in the circuitry, and it and a transmitter were placed in a twelve-inch-square box. The transmitter was attached to a telephone receiver and batteries. Melton acknowledged that the redesigned device still worked better when operated by a medium but said that nonetheless he himself had received spirit voices through it.

Melton claimed that researchers all over the world contacted him for more information, and the College of Psychic Science in London championed his work. In actuality, few seemed to have taken much notice.

About a decade later, the American psychical researcher Hereward Carrington came across Melton's work and was intrigued enough to try to replicate his results. Carrington built a psychic telephone but added his own modifications to Melton's plan. Carrington's experiments failed, and the device fell into obscurity.

At about the same time that Melton was experimenting with his device, author and medium Francis Grierson (who went by the name of Jesse Shepard when working as a medium) invented a "psychophone." He said he received messages from the dead through it and privately published his results. Few copies circulated and even fewer have survived, and little is known about this device.

More psychic telephones appeared, some of them rising from and falling beneath the waves in short order. In 1947 a Dutch researcher named N. Zwann said he had received mediumistic communications from spirits who had given him plans to build a psychic telephone. Zwann went to England in search of technical help. A device was built, and Zwann claimed success—but he never gave any public demonstrations to back up his claims.

Another device was created in the 1940s by Harry Gardner and J. Gilbert Wright, who combined their Spiritualist interests and technical expertise. Their device was less like a telephone and more like an amplifier of direct spirit voices produced by a medium, much like the old-fashioned simple trumpets of the old Spiritualist days. The device was a box measuring twenty-four by seven inches, lined with soundproofing and drilled with a small hole on one side. A microphone was placed inside and was connected via the hole to an external loudspeaker. When placed next to a medium, the device seemed to amplify spirit voices. The inventors improved their device by making it magnetic with the addition of iron in a puttylike material to the lining of the box.

Intriguing as these devices were, none of them ever achieved any wide success or application. Edison's alleged device never made a public appearance, and the rest of the contenders worked so quirkily, if at all, that they failed to capture much attention. High-tech spirit communications progressed in other directions beyond telephones to the dead.

6

The Birth of Electronic Voice Phenomena

Edison's invention of the phonograph in 1877 paved the way for Electronic Voice Phenomena, the recording of unknown voices. In his early models, sound waves were recorded by a sewing machine needle etching a wax cylinder and played back through a trumpet. You have probably seen the famous logo of a dog seated by a turntable with a large megaphone attached. Among the first words that Edison boomed into his machine for public demonstration was a nursery rhyme, "Mary's Little Lamb."

To a late-nineteenth-century audience, the phonograph seemed miraculous, even beyond credibility, just as some of our modern spirit communications devices seem today.

Some of Edison's most learned peers did not believe what they saw and heard. One scientist declared that he had examined the phonograph and it was nothing more than a trick of ventriloquism. It soon became apparent that no such trickery was involved. Even more astonishing was evidence that the phonograph could record the voices of mysterious "others."

The very first known recording of spirit voices happened around 1901. Waldemar Borogas, an exile to Siberia, studied the shamanic practices of a remote Siberian tribe, the Tchouktchis. During a conjuring ritual, the shaman rhythmically beat his drum to enter a trance. Borogas listened in amazement as the space around them became filled with disembodied voices, as though invisible spirits were joining in the ritual. Borogas had a portable Edison phonograph, and he thought perhaps he could record the spirits' voices on it. At another ritual, he set it up. The shaman asked the communicators to speak directly into the phonograph and they evidently obliged, for Borogas captured not only the unknown voices he heard but others that were not heard at the time as well.

The first systematic EVP experiments were done in the 1930s by Attila von Szalay, an American photographer who also had psychic ability. He was motivated by personal experience: in 1938 he heard a voice in the air near him exclaiming, "Art!" that he thought belonged to his dead son, Edson. The voice, and other voices, continued to manifest in the air around Attila, especially after he meditated or did yoga. Von Szalay recorded mystery voices first onto 78 rpm records and then onto magnetic recorders, which were introduced in the 1920s.

Von Szalay teamed up with Raymond Bayless in 1956 to conduct more experiments with voices. They worked together until 1975; psychical researcher D. Scott Rogo joined them in 1968. (Bayless and Rogo went on to research phone calls from the dead, which we mentioned in our opening chapter.)

Bayless and von Szalay rented a studio in Hollywood and constructed a cabinet, much like those used in Spiritualist séances. Von Szalay sat inside the cabinet and tried to produce the direct voices. An aluminum trumpet with a microphone in the bell was placed inside the cabinet, and a magnetic tape recorder was placed outside it. Recordings were made of mysterious male and female voices, whistles, and raps, which came out of the trumpet even when von Szalay was outside the cabinet. If von Szalay whistled, the voices whistled back. The recorder also picked up unheard voices.

The voices answered specific questions, called out proper names, and even uttered profanity. Over the course of time, the results improved. The first voices spoke an average of five to seven words. That increased to fifteen words and then recordings that lasted up to forty-five seconds in length—an exceptional length of time by even today's average EVP results.

FRIEDRICH JÜRGENSON TUNES IN THE DEAD

Electronic Voice Phenomena got a better boost in the 1960s when Friedrich Jürgenson, a Latvian-born-turned-Swedish-citizen opera singer, painter, and film producer, published a book about his tape recordings of spirit voices, *The Inaudible Becomes Audible*, also published as *The Voices from Space* (1964). A record of voice recordings accompanied the book.

Jürgenson did much more than record unknown voices. He was probably the first major high-tech spirit communications researcher to undergo a profound spiritual transformation as a result of his work. Jürgenson found himself catapulted into a metaphysical realm that stretched his ideas about life and death, the nature of the human soul, and the interconnections of all things in creation. Like Tesla, he conceived of sweeping visions for the raising up of humanity. He would have plenty of company in this regard as others joined in research on down the road. Researcher-turned-mystic became a common theme in spirit communications.

At the time of Jürgenson's breakthrough, the term "Electronic Voice Phenomena" hadn't been coined yet. The voices were simply "voices" or "spirit voices" or "unknown voices." Jürgenson called his disembodied communicators "friends."

Jürgenson said he accidentally discovered the voices in 1959 while trying to record birdsongs in the Swedish countryside near his villa at Mölnbo. On the sunny afternoon of June 12, he and his wife headed out to a favorite lake. Jürgenson, who had been interested in birdsongs since childhood, took along his tape recorder, intending to set it up at a small hut by the lake. At about 4:00 P.M. he went into the attic and set his recorder and microphone near an open window. When a finch appeared, Jürgenson turned the recorder on and let it run about five minutes. When he listened to his recording, he was puzzled. The sounds of birds chirping were muffled by a hissing and roaring, followed by a trumpetlike sound, followed by a male voice speaking in Norwegian about "birdsongs at night."

Jürgenson had heard only the bird chirping as he recorded. At first, he thought he had picked up a stray radio broadcast—except there was no radio on and there were no radio stations even within receiving distance of their location. He thought it especially strange that a man would discuss birdsongs at the precise time Jürgenson was trying to record them.

Inspired to experiment further, he made other birdsong recordings and got more strange voices, which he never heard during recording but only on playback. Even more intriguing, the voices had personal information for him, plus they gave him instructions on how to record more voices. "Friedrich, you are being watched," he was told once. Another time, he heard his mother, who had been dead for four years, speak to him using her nickname for him: "Friedel, my little Friedel, can you hear me?"

Then he began to hear the voices in real time as he listened to the radio while wearing headphones, but the best results still were obtained on playback. A signature of the mysterious transmissions was a loud hissing noise. Some of the communicators spoke in strange hissing voices, too. One of them was a female who identified herself as Lena; she became his "mediator," assisting his research.

By July 1960, transmissions were flooding in on a daily basis. The voices took over his life. Jürgenson listened to all of them, logged them into notebooks, and laboriously transcribed them. He gave up his professional career and devoted himself to studying the voices. After eight years, he had amassed between five and six thousand recordings and twenty logbooks of notes. He had heard from dozens of dead family members and friends whose voices he recognized and had received communications from dozens of prominent and famous people as well. He had experimented with a variety of techniques, including getting voices directly over the radio. The research, he said, was "the most fascinating work of my life."

Jürgenson held a press conference in 1963 to reveal his research, fully expecting to be ridiculed. Some did laugh, but others took his news quite seriously, for they had been privately doing the same kind of research. Jürgenson was contacted by numerous individuals who had similar experiences and also by others whose curiosity was aroused.

By the time he published his first book, after eight years of research, Jürgenson felt profoundly changed in mind, body, and spirit. He believed that because of his musical training, sensitive ear, and fluency in five languages he had been "selected by some unknown force to be a pioneer and at the same time to be a humble guinea pig also forced to endure with body and soul a considerable measure of stress and challenge." He confessed that initially he had questioned his sanity and wondered if he were descending into schizophrenia. After about two years, stability restored itself and he found himself on a new plane of thought. He felt he had emerged onto the cutting edge of a new era of humanity. The tapes proved to him that he was not imagining the voices. "As far as I know, this form of knowledge is absolutely new in the history of mankind as known to us," he said.

THE RAUDIVE VOICES

Although Jürgenson was by no means the first person to experiment with Electronic Voice Phenomena, his work later earned him the title of The Father of the Electronic Voice Phenomenon. He inspired another giant in the EVP field: Konstantin Raudive, a Latvian psychologist and philosopher. Raudive, a student of Carl G. Jung, taught at Uppsala University in Sweden. He was interested in parapsychology, psychical research, and survival after death. Intrigued by Jürgenson's recordings and convinced of his sincerity, Raudive arranged to meet him in 1965. Jürgenson did demonstrations for Raudive and others that produced clear voices. When one of the researchers remarked that she thought that people in the afterlife were living a happy, carefree life, a disembodied voice answered, "Nonsense!" Apparently the dead have their dramas and problems, too!

Raudive did his best to find natural explanations for the voices but could not. He became convinced that the "voices of mysterious origin," as he called them, were genuine. He plunged into his own research, experimenting with three techniques:

- Microphone voices, obtained by leaving a tape recorder running by itself.
- Radio voices, obtained with white noise generated between stations.
- Diode voices, obtained with a crystal set not tuned to a station.

Getting results was not easy. Three months passed before Raudive heard his first voice, a male who responded in Latvian, "That is right," to Raudive's observation that the dead have to contend with limitations in communications, too. As he continued, he discovered what other researchers have found—that one develops an ear for hearing spirit voices that improves with practice. When he listened again to his early tapes, he found that his recorder had captured many voices that he had not been able to discern the first time around. After another three months, his own spirit mediator appeared, a female who gave her name as Spidola.

Raudive found that radio produced the best spirit voices.

He did his own prototype of a "ghost box" by manually and slowly moving his radio tuner dial up the broadcast band until he heard a voice say, "Now!" or, "Make recording!" or something similar. Then he turned on his tape recorder. On playback, he heard voices that stood out from the radio noise.

The spirit voices could be distinguished from ordinary radio voices by their paranormal features, such as peculiar rhythms and speech patterns. They spoke directly to him, gave their names, offered personal information, and gave advice on his techniques. Raudive made about one hundred thousand recordings of electronic voices speaking in words and phrases in different languages. Some were clear and others sounded like bad long-distance telephone connections. Some of the words and phrases were understandable, while others seemed to be masked in code. Sometimes only one or two voices spoke; at other times a multitude of voices spoke in jumbles.

He established a classification system for the voices: Class A are clear and easy to understand, Class B are less distinct but can be understood by a trained ear, and Class C are faint and usually require headphones and, in modern times, perhaps software manipulation in order to make them out.

Raudive published his research in German in 1968 in his book *The Inaudible Made Audible*. His work was so influential that the term "Raudive voices" became the norm.

In 1971 an English publisher, Colin Smythe, became intrigued by Raudive's work and asked psychologist and

Cambridge scholar Peter Bander to translate it into English for publication. Bander's initial reaction was negative. As he later put it, ". . . the thought of dead people communicating through a tape recorder seemed really too silly to be taken seriously."

Colin Smythe himself, the namesake of his publishing company, thought otherwise and decided to test Raudive's method. Smythe recorded a female voice that to him was meaningless. He persuaded Bander to give it a listen. Bander reluctantly agreed, convinced that whatever Smythe heard was in his imagination.

When Bander listened to the tape, he got a shock. The voice was that of his mother, who had died three years earlier! Speaking in German, she said, "Why don't you open the door?" It was a double entendre, a reference to Bander's habit of keeping the door to his office closed and also to opening the door to Raudive's work. Bander not only changed his mind about publishing Raudive's book—he also became one of the leading spokespeople for spirit voices himself, conducting his own research and writing his own books on the subject.

A NEW FRONTIER

Bander and Smythe coined the term "Electronic Voice Phenomenon." EVP research swept around the world. Some researchers started as skeptics to disprove Electronic Voice Phenomena and became converts themselves.

One skeptic was Sarah Estep, an American housewife

who set up a reel-to-reel tape recorder in the basement of her Maryland home every night in 1976 to debunk the notion that voices of the dead would talk to her. In her belief, death was final—there was no afterlife. She had known this since childhood. Her grandparents had owned a funeral home in Westfield, New York. On summer visits, little Sarah would sneak into the viewing rooms and peer into the caskets to look at the dead. It seemed clear to her that death was a casket—after you died, away you went, into a box and into the ground. And that was the end of you.

In 1976 Estep read about Electronic Voice Phenomena and the work of Jürgenson, Raudive, and others. They must be wrong! How could the dead communicate when there was no afterlife? To her, Electronic Voice Phenomena were tricks of the mind, a way to ease the fears of the living about the finality of death. She decided she would prove it to herself by trying Electronic Voice Phenomena, convinced she would get no communication.

Night after night, she started up the recorder, asked the same questions, and left space for answers: "Is anyone here? . . . Please tell me your name . . . Where are you? . . . Can you hear me?" Every morning, she reviewed her tapes. After nearly a week of staggering boredom and no answers, Estep was on her last night of experiments. If nothing happened on this night, she would cease Electronic Voice Phenomena and remain comfortable in her conviction of no survival after death.

As she reviewed her tape the next morning, she got the

shock of her life. Following her question "Please tell me what your world is like," a clear female voice said, "Beauty."

Estep played the segment over and over. There was no mistaking it. The answer was not her imagination. Suddenly the impact swept over her. She, Sarah Estep, sitting in her basement in Maryland, had somehow connected with a being from another world!

It was almost too much to absorb, and for a time Estep vacillated between belief and doubt. At first doubt won and she decided that "Beauty" was a freak accident. She kept recording, but instead of more voices, she was greeted with silence again. Frustrated after nearly a month without results, she was once again on the brink of quitting.

Then came some encouraging messages: "Don't give up" and "Keep it up." Estep followed the guidance. It still took her about six months to get enough messages to convince herself there might be an afterlife. It took six years to get a message that sealed it for her once and for all. One night, a communicator somberly announced, "Death no more a casket." Another shock went through Estep. She had the feeling that whoever they were, the communicators knew about her childhood habit of peeking into caskets at her grandparents' funeral home.

The messages brought a complete upheaval of her beliefs about life and death. She had done her own experiments and heard proof that she could not deny. Were the voices speaking from the afterlife or from some planet in the far reaches of the universe? There was no way to know for sure, but clearly, other beings or people were out there.

In 1982, with thousands of Electronic Voice Phenomena now in her vault, Estep founded the American Association of Electronic Voice Phenomena (AA-EVP) and became a world leader in the study of Electronic Voice Phenomena. Rosemary became acquainted with Estep during the years they both lived in the Annapolis area. Estep kept her reel-to-reel setup in her office, ready to go. Every now and then, Rosemary would visit. They talked about Electronic Voice Phenomena, listened to some of Estep's archived recordings, and turned on the reel-to-reel to capture fresh voices over a radio tuned to the aircraft band for background noise.

Until around 2000, Estep recorded daily and received an average of three to four messages a day. By then she had twenty-five thousand Electronic Voice Phenomena. Of those, she judged about twenty-two thousand to be communications with the dead, two thousand with extraterrestrials, and one thousand with beings who lived in other dimensions. In 2000 she retired from the AA-EVP and turned its direction over to Tom and Lisa Butler of Reno, Nevada. The Butlers renamed the organization the Association TransCommunication (ATransC) in 2010 to reflect the broadening scope of spirit communications researchers.

One of Estep's most startling EVP communications came from a male communicator who announced, "I live." If the afterlife is life, she asked, then what did he think of his physical life on Earth? "Death!" he exclaimed.

"I believe this must be true," Estep said in her last

book, *Roads to Eternity* (2005). "Not that what we are experiencing now is death (for there is no physical death, only death of imperfect ideas), but while we think we may be living a more or less full life at this time, it can't begin to compare with what we will find when we take our final road to eternity."

Estep said that one of the most important messages she ever received in Electronic Voice Phenomena was "Your soul is not defeated." She found great reassurance in the soul continuing on. She believed that the good and the negative acts committed during life determine what we find on the Other Side. However, future lifetimes, through reincarnation, would always provide opportunities for learning and growth.

This good and gentle person passed into the afterlife herself on January 6, 2008. Rosemary and Tom and Lisa were among those who attended Estep's funeral in Annapolis. Like other researchers who have gone before her, she is reported to communicate in Electronic Voice Phenomena. Brazilian researcher Sonia Rinaldi has recorded Estep on a number of occasions, uttering short replies to questions, such as "I hear" and "Now good-bye."

LIVE AND REAL TIME

Even while people such as Estep were hauling out their tape recorders to capture passive Electronic Voice Phenomena, the dead were talking in live two-way exchanges to researchers. Both Jürgenson and Raudive had already found ways to communicate live.

Jürgenson got the idea to plug his tape recorder directly into a radio receiver. A woman's voice announced: "Through the radio . . . you have guessed it . . . much more will come through . . ." The vibration of her voice moved him to the core of his being. He suddenly realized that radio had tremendous potential for bridging worlds. He didn't know exactly how, but he vowed he would find out.

Jürgenson educated himself on radio frequencies and transmitters. He now called his "friends" the "broadcasting station of the deceased." He noticed certain characteristics. He often got messages when he turned on his radio at the end of the day but rarely got messages past ten o'clock at night or while he was concentrating on writing his book. He also noticed other patterns. There were no transmissions on shortwave frequencies, during news broadcasts, or during solar flare activity and northern lights displays. Transmissions abruptly ended right before thunderstorms began.

His female mediator, Lena, guided him with how to use sound frequencies to improve his results. She was always right and so he followed her instructions to the letter.

Lena spoke rapidly, using a special frequency that she created from the overlapping of certain sounds. Unless a person had an attunement to Electronic Voice Phenomena acquired from years of listening, he would hear this frequency only as a "toneless, meaningless hissing." Jürgenson discovered that his spirit communicators were able to turn any background sound into words, even the barking of a dog.

I have to digress for a moment, because I am reminded of a caller who asked me one night, "Hey, George, have you ever heard of the Coffee Pot Ghost?"

"The Coffee Pot Ghost? A ghost who looks like a coffeepot? Or a ghost who *is* a coffeepot?" I said jokingly.

"There's this woman—you can read about her on the Internet—who says that spirits can talk to her through the gurgling of her coffeepot when she makes coffee," he said.

"I don't know if I'd like spirits talking to me while I'm trying to wake up with my coffee," I said. "You know, I'm already out here on the edge with my guests every night. If I start hearing voices from the coffeepot, someone might want to cart me away."

"Well, it's no joke," the caller said. "It's for real. You should check it out."

"Thanks for the tip," I said.

Sure enough, we later found the Coffee Pot Ghost. It seems the soft sounds of percolating coffee made just the right backdrop of noise to produce spirit voices. A further search revealed that people have heard spirit voices coming from the sounds of electric shavers (which happened to Jürgenson) and hair dryers, vacuum cleaners, water fountains, air conditioners, and so on. It sounds crazy, but EVP researchers do confirm that almost any steady background noise can do the trick.

Raudive figured this out, too. He experimented with setups of tape recorders, microphones, and radios to get live voices and got his best results when the radio was tuned to white noise.

THE PSYCHOFON REVOLUTION

The man who really invented the first "ghost box" for live, two-way spirit talk was a Viennese electrical engineer by the name of Franz Seidl. He developed an instrument that enabled deaf people to hear, even some who had been deaf from birth. The instrument sent a tone-modulated high frequency into the brain. Intrigued to experiment in Electronic Voice Phenomena, Seidl combined tone-modulated high frequencies and the radio to create a unique device he called the Psychofon. Instead of tuning a radio steadily to white noise between stations, the Psychofon rapidly scanned the radio bandwidth.

Seidl is not well-known in English-speaking countries because little of his work was translated, but we believe he deserves more attention. Like other great contributors to the field, he was ahead of his time in understanding the process of spirit communications, not only from a technical perspective but from a more subtle spiritual perspective as well.

"I have a great respect for Seidl," Rosemary told me during a conversation we had about our research. "He experienced everything that the users of ghost boxes experience today. And he was right in in his conclusions about the process of spirit communications."

In 1959 Seidl acquired a tape recorder and started

taping animal and bird sounds as a hobby. Something peculiar happened during many of the recording sessions. When he played his tapes back, every now and then he heard a human voice that he was sure had not been audible during the taping. He could not understand any of the voices. Then during one listening session he was hit with a voice that electrified him. Unmistakably, he heard his dead mother calling his name. Further experimentation convinced Seidl that somehow the dead were communicating through the heads on the recorder.

Seidl's Psychofon is not to be confused with the Psycho-Phone, invented by A. B. Salinger in the 1920s. Salinger's Psycho-Phone was a commercial device for subliminal programming during sleep. No claims were made of paranormal possibilities. Psycho-Phones surface from time to time in estate sales and auctions, and sometimes buyers think they have acquired a genuine prototype of a spirit telephone, perhaps even the legendary one said to have been created by Edison. Not so; as we noted earlier, there are no known surviving Edison prototypes—if any were ever made in the first place.

Seidl believed he had discovered a new form of "transcendental physics," which he called Psitronik. "Psychofonie" was his term for research involving the new method of recording paranormal voices. Seidl said that paranormal voices could not be explained by classical physics because "in other dimensions there exist different rules of nature which are beyond our space-time continuum."

The hearing of "voices from beyond the grave" was not a hallucination or hoax, he said. "All one has to do is listen and hear and they will know the truth . . . [T]here are other planes of existence where people like us and not like us may live and perhaps want to communicate with us."

Seidl found that results were not entirely dependent on the device but were heavily dependent on the cooperation of the spirit communicators and the "mental readiness" of the living experimenter. Psychic ability influenced results, and so did preparing for a session by meditating first.

Believers got better results than nonbelievers. "When you believe, you open all possibilities," he said. As for disbelievers, he stated, "Some deny the existence of the soul. Thus they can't believe in life after death, so they reject the idea that souls who are not here can still talk with us. Of these people they will often claim that they are hearing signals from some broadcasting corporation. These people are so closed that if [paranormal] voices fell on their head they would not know it."

Paranormal voices, like "standard" EVP voices, are distinctly different from anything coming from the radio broadcast, Seidl said. With practice, listeners learn to distinguish the difference. He believed that a "mental synchronization" among the listeners present would help the dead to form words. "If several persons in mental synchronization give more energy to the signal, a special loading condition will arise and produce a kind of field collapse in the radio signal. . . . A transformation of this kind of energy into an electromagnetic wave may allow these voices to be received or taped."

Seidl cautioned that results may not be immediate and there seemed to be a natural optimum window of communication. "You cannot lose patience when no contact takes place at once," he said. "It may take a long time for conditions to be correct. Communications normally start ten minutes into the session and peak at thirty minutes, then start to fade. Location and time of day play an important part in communication. One cannot force a spirit or entity to talk with you or give you a message."

Seidl began experimenting with photography during his taping sessions and discovered that he had "extras" in some of his photographs. An extra is an unknown image or figure, believed to be a spirit or a dead person. The extras are not seen visually but show up on the image.

Seidl's work led to profound psychic and spiritual experiences. He experienced levitation, and he became interested in researching the consciousness or souls of plants. He died in 1982. His best-known work is *The Phenomenon of Transcendental Voices* (1971), but it was not as widely translated as the works of Jürgenson and Raudive. Seidl's schematics are available on the Internet today, and experimenters still follow them to build devices. Few outside Europe today, however, recognize the name of this man, one of the most significant inventors in the field of spirit communications.

THE KOENIG GENERATOR

One other major influence on the development of real-time Electronic Voice Phenomena was Hans Otto Koenig, a German electronics engineer. Like many of the researchers in Electronic Voice Phenomena, Koenig entered the field in the early 1970s as a skeptic, and he had tried to debunk Electronic Voice Phenomena with his own experiments. Instead of debunking the voices, he heard the voice of his dead mother and some friends and acquaintances.

Convinced that he was indeed taping voices of the dead, Koenig sought to go beyond that into real-time, two-way communication. He experimented with background noises, such as radio static and running water. He realized that these noises contained ultrasonic sounds above the range of tape recorders, which do not pick up sounds higher than 20KHz. He thought that spirit communication might occur mostly in the ultrasonic range and spent about eight years developing equipment that would reach into 30KHz, far beyond the hearing ability of the human ear. He achieved a communications bridge in 1981.

Koenig called his invention "Koenig's generator." The generator was actually a combination of four sound generators that mixed fixed ultrasonic frequencies with warble generator ultrasonic frequencies, which in turn created an audible sound resembling a police car siren but with a constantly changing frequency. According to Koenig, the spirit signals heterodyned with the multifrequency energy of the generator and were transposed into audible sounds.

On January 15, 1983, Koenig went live on Radio Luxembourg with his generator to demonstrate real-time spirit communications. The audience was in the millions. It was risky, but Koenig was ultraconfident his equipment would be successful. Questions would be posed by the station staff. As the program got under way, one staffer asked if there was anyone from the Other Side who could speak. Within a few seconds a clear voice said, "Otto Koenig makes wireless with the dead." A response to another question was, "We hear your voice." Every question received a clear and direct response. Even the deceased Raudive showed up, and the voice matched other recordings of Raudive while he was alive. By the end of the broadcast, the host, Rainer Holbe, was obviously shaken. He said tremulously, "I swear by the life of my children that nothing has been manipulated. There are no tricks. It is a voice and we do not know from where it comes."

Koenig kept experimenting and built other setups that yielded longer exchanges with less distortion. He conducted controlled experiments at different locations, eventually achieving a high level of real-time communications. Researchers from around the world came to see his generators perform and went away convinced that Koenig indeed had summoned up the dead.

7

Who Are We Talking To?

The haunted ruins of the Waverly Hills Sanatorium in Louisville, Kentucky, seem like an odd place to meet up with your dead grandmother, a kindly woman who loved to bake you cookies and who never once set foot in the sprawling former tuberculosis facility. But the paranormal is full of strange events like this and stranger things still.

Waverly Hills, a favorite with paranormal investigators because of its haunting activity, seemed like a perfect place for Bill Chappell to run some tests on his Paranormal Puck. In the midst of a session, the words "tennis shoes" appeared on the computer screen and then the word "cookie." Suddenly a woman who was in the group observing the Puck in action burst into tears.

Concerned, Chappell went immediately to her. "What's wrong?" he asked.

"That's my grandmother coming through," the woman sobbed.

"Your grandmother? How do you know?"

"She always wore tennis shoes," the woman said. "And she baked us cookies."

The description probably could fit many grandmothers, and the words alone don't necessarily prove that a certain deceased grandmother was present, somehow beaming in from the Beyond to the dark, scary corridors of Waverly. But to the woman present it was proof positive that her grandmother had reached out and made contact through the wonders of technology. Grandma had nothing more to say that night, at least nothing that could be captured on this side. But it was enough for her granddaughter, who went home with a gift beyond price—the comfort that somewhere out there in space and time Grandma carried on.

The overwhelming majority of spirit communications obtained through technology fall into a subjective category, in which one or more listeners feel they just "know" who is coming through. They recognize a voice, an accent, a choice of words, some facts. We've already seen how the conviction of voices of dead loved ones galvanized researchers such as Konstantin Raudive, Attila von Szalay, Peter Bander, and others. The proof of the identity is often highly personal, depending on the recognition of a voice or use of nicknames, favorite expressions, or intimate information that reveals an identity.

Assuming we are getting genuine communication, how can we prove who we are talking to? Sometimes the communicators give a name or say who or what they are but offer little else. We have no idea whether that is deliberate or a shortcoming in the technology. Probably we are getting only a fraction of what is being transmitted to us. But without better links, we on this side are left with the choice—perhaps "dilemma" is a better word—of whether or not to take the communicators at face value.

PORTALS AND WORMHOLES

Where exactly are communicators located? The most likely explanation is that they reside in a parallel dimension or perhaps even a parallel universe. Parallel dimensions are other realms that exist in our universe but are invisible to us. Parallel universes are separate universes that are very close to our universe. Parallel dimensions connect to us through portals; parallel universes connect through wormholes.

These parallel realms are supported in physics by M theory, formerly known as string theory. According to this theory, the smallest units of matter are two-dimensional vibrating strings, not particles. Strings can be open or closed, and their vibrations determine the building blocks of the universe. The strings are attached to a membrane—called a "brane" by scientists—which is like a web of space and time that ties everything together. There are an infinite number of branes, some of which have different laws of physics from ours.

Scientists think there are eleven dimensions in each universe, or brane. We live in the third dimension, but we can't see it because we are attached to it and it moves when we do; and it is extremely close to us—perhaps several hundred trillionths of a millimeter. We normally cannot see or even enter the other dimensions because they exist at angles to us and are folded around our dimension; we would have to bend space in order to perceive them. Physicists used to believe that these dimensions were tiny in size, on the level of the nucleus of an atom, but now many think they are quite large.

Our own brane or universe encompasses all the planets, stars, and galaxies that we can see. A parallel universe is another brane with its own dimensions, planets, stars, and galaxies. Other branes vary in size. Some are quite distant from us in space and time, while others are close—perhaps close enough to interact with our brane.

Our spirit communications may take place when *portals* open up between dimensions due to a bending of space that overlaps two strings and to the opening of *wormholes*, or tunnels, when two universes come close enough to interact with each other and connect. The openings might allow energy and matter—one or the other or both—to flow between realities. If the beings on the other side have the right technology, they may be able to penetrate our dimension or brane.

The amount of energy required to open a wormhole is tremendous, so, most likely, the communicators we contact are in parallel dimensions, reached through portals that open up in the Earth's magnetosphere under the right conditions, according to Philip J. Imbrogno, a science educator who has pursued study of ufology, interdimensional contact, and spirit communications.

Could spirit communicators create portals? Perhaps—some of them do talk about manipulating energy on their side. Our communications devices, such as radio sweep boxes, might help the process, too. "If you have a device that is emitting a particular oscillator frequency and there is someone in a close parallel reality who is doing the same thing, their oscillator is going to lock onto your oscillator," Imbrogno told us.

The Other Side or the afterlife would be a parallel dimension to ours. Who knows who lives in the other dimensions around us? The following sections provide descriptions of some of our spirit communicators.

THEY KNOW US; WE DON'T KNOW THEM

Some communicators give names, but the experimenters do not know them personally. Are they dead people who have found a portal for communication? Sometimes they seem to know us or at least know who we are.

Rosemary had such an encounter with spirit communicators during an investigation of the haunted Lincoln Square Theatre in Decatur, Illinois, where Houdini once performed. Her MiniBox sessions were videotaped by Joey Tito of the Ghost Research Society of Chicago.

In the basement, Rosemary opened the session by asking if there was anyone who wanted to communicate. "Can you identify anyone in the room here?" Rosemary asked.

A faint male voice responded, "Joey . . . uh-huh."

"Do you know Joey?" Rosemary said. "There is a Joey in the theater."

The male voice answered, "That's him."

"Do you know Joey?" Rosemary repeated, looking for validation.

"Yes, I do," the communicator said.

"It's him?" Rosemary said.

A female voice broke in. "Joey . . . yes . . . It's him."

Multiple voices chimed in, "It's him."

And that was it. The voices disappeared. Who were these communicators and how did they know Joey Tito? The mystery remains.

Rosemary moved the box to another spot in the basement and started a new session. Within a few moments, a gender-neutral voice said, "Question."

Rosemary said, "Would anyone like to ask a question?"

A high-pitched female voice announced, "I'm here."

"Someone said, 'I'm here.' Who's here?" Rosemary replied.

A male voice answered, "Everybody's here," followed by a female voice saying, "Rachel."

"Rachel? Rachel, do you know anyone in the room?" Rosemary asked.

"Author," the voice responded. It was tinny and fragmented, like "auth-or."

"Why is Rachel here in the theater?" Rosemary asked.

The voice responded, "Rosemary."

Again, the conversation terminated just as it was getting interesting. Rosemary was puzzled, for she knows no person named Rachel who had gone into the afterlife. Is it possible Rosemary and other listeners did not hear the name correctly? Or is there a person—or entity—with that name, or using that name, who knows Rosemary and was able to get through? Did the communicators end the transmission—or was a connection lost on one or both sides?

Sometimes the communicators indicate that they can see us or hear and see things going on in our environment, even though we cannot see them. The effect can be a bit unnerving at times.

At Waverly Hills, Bill Chappell had another strange experience with the Paranormal Puck. While he was running the equipment, another researcher, a man, tripped and fell, making a loud sound. A voice on the Puck said, "What fell?"

SOMETIMES THEY TALK TO EACH OTHER AND NOT TO US

Every now and then, the listeners on this side feel more like eavesdroppers than communicators. We think our devices are intended to connect us to other realms—but they also let us drop in on conversations that don't involve us.

Ron Ricketts, the creator of the MiniBox, once was totally taken aback when two apparently discarnate men began talking to each other instead of to the living. Ricketts was with a group of people who made contact with a male voice and repeatedly asked him to identify himself. Another male voice broke through, saying, "George, is that you?"

Only static sounded for a few moments, and then the original communicator hesitantly answered back, "Frank? Frank, this is George!"

More static.

"George!" exclaimed the voice identifying itself as Frank.

"Frank!" exclaimed George. "I thought you were dead!"

"I am!" answered Frank.

Then nothing. The entire conversation terminated—or, more likely, it carried on somewhere in the ethers beyond the ability of the equipment to pick it up.

"I was dumbfounded," Ricketts said. "We had two discarnate entities having a rational conversation with each other. I was watching the scan on the MiniBox—they were on opposite bands from each other. They were definitely *not* two guys on the same radio station."

Sarah Estep took a trip to Egypt and did Electronic Voice Phenomena wherever she went, including the pyramids at Giza. At the base of the Great Pyramid, she conducted a session with her tape recorder, asking questions. Apparently there was a debate among the communicators about responding to her, for on playback Estep heard a voice ask, "Can she be trusted?" referring to Estep. Another voice answered, "Yes, she is a good person." For the remainder of Estep's stay, she received many EVP communications.

Finally, we have an odd case that falls under the "mind your manners" category. Apparently, even those in other dimensions have rules of courtesy. Every researcher has experienced abusive communicators who use foul language and threats. They should be told to go away, and if they don't the session should be ended.

One of Rosemary's investigations involved a haunted former hotel occupied by a ghostly presence dubbed Stinky. The name is appropriate, for the ghost has a foul appearance, a foul smell—and a foul mouth. Stinky likes to abuse investigators. He made no exception on Rosemary's first visit, arranged by Al Brinzda, co-founder of the Allegheny Mountain Ghosthunters.

The investigators set up Rosemary's Frank's Box number 45 in the room where Stinky was most often encountered. He made himself immediately known, answering their questions with insults, obscenities, and threats. This was Stinky's modus operandi, and the investigators decided to let the session run awhile to see if he would wind down. In the midst of his rant, a cool male voice interrupted, saying, "Just be polite."

It did no good, however. Stinky continued on, and Rosemary shut the box off. But who was Mr. Manners and why was he eavesdropping? We will never know!

PULLING YOUR LEG

Sometimes it seems obvious that communicators are play-ing jokes and having fun with us. It is difficult, if not im-possible, to know who or what is behind some of these trickster pranks, but they give us evidence in a peculiar way that is hard to dismiss.

Just about everyone who works in the paranormal soon comes face-to-face with Trickster. In mythologies, Trickster is the god who portrays and embodies the forces of chaos and destruction. He is a clever, sneaky character who swings easily from being a good guy to a mean and nasty guy, and he loves to have a belly laugh at your expense.

In the paranormal, Trickster can be either a force or an entity that strikes with such things as the failure of fresh batteries and equipment (usually at a crucial moment), bizarre phenomena, and events that suddenly go twisted and awry—all without explanation.

Both Rosemary and I have had a good share of Trick-ster phenomena over the years, no matter what we're fo-cused on: ghosts, UFOs, aliens, crypto-creatures, shadow people—in short, any phenomena or entities in the super-natural. Rosemary had a striking Trickster experience one evening while investigating the haunted West Virginia State Penitentiary in Moundsville. Now a historic site, Mounds-ville, as the Gothic-style prison is known, is another favor-ite in the paranormal community. The prison was the scene of some of the most bloody and violent events in U.S. prison history. It is a favorite with paranormal investigators. As with Waverly, it is hard *not* to have experiences and get evidence when visiting there.

First, remember that radio sweep boxes, if set properly, do not produce stretches of music or conversation. You will hear a note or two or a word or two as the scan moves past a station.

Rosemary was working with two investigators, Scott Philips and Maureen Davis, from the Center for Paranormal Study and Investigation, based in the Pittsburgh, Pennsylvania, area. They set up their equipment—including the MiniBox—in various spots. Some nights are more active than others, and this night was paranormally "hot." You can even feel it in the air—there is an almost electrical quality to the environment, a "vibe" that experienced investigators appreciate. Throughout the evening, a lot had come through on the box, and the investigators had also experienced apparitions and thumpings and bangings where they had set up.

At the end of the night, they made their way to their last spot, the Sugar Shack, one of the prison's famous paranormal hot spots. The basement Sugar Shack was used for recreation when the weather was severe. Supervision was lax, and inmates engaged in violence and certain "recreational" activities.

They set up their equipment with high expectations for this last session. They were quickly disappointed. A few minutes into it, they felt the room go "flat." Nothing came over the box in response to questions.

After a few minutes, the MiniBox suddenly went silent.

It hadn't been touched. Rosemary examined it and found that somehow the volume knob had been turned all the way down. The tampering with equipment by invisible means is a common experience in haunting investigations. She readjusted the volume, and the box resumed its scan.

After a few more minutes, the MiniBox cut out again. She examined it and found that this time the speaker jack was pulled partway out—not completely but enough to cut the audio. She pushed the jack back in and the scan sound resumed. Exasperated, she commented to Scott and Maureen about what had happened twice—as though "someone" was playing with the MiniBox equipment.

Rosemary said out loud into the dark room, "Is that you?"

Nothing responded over the Mini, which scanned away in a jumble of radio noise.

Maureen said, "You don't want to talk to us, do you?"

Rosemary repeated, "Is that you? Are you messing with our equipment?"

Without a beat, an answer came over the Mini—a long and sustained portion of the theme music from *The Twilight Zone*.

The three of them burst out laughing. They had gotten an answer to their questions, in effect, "Yes, that is me [or us] playing with your equipment, and *you* are in the Twilight Zone!"

We played that clip one night on *Coast to Coast*. It remains one of the strangest communications Rosemary has obtained in her work in spirit communications. Was it a ghost of a former inmate? A trickster entity? Someone or something else? Whoever or whatever it was, it had a sense of humor comparable to ours.

Chappell has had his share of bizarre and humorous communications as well. One came while he was at work on a new device called the Talker, which generates phonetic speech without software programming. Instead, the speech generation is caused by energy values, such as ionization in the air. One day Chappell had the Talker sitting on his workbench. The device piped up and a robotic voice said, "Billy." Pause. "Billy."

Chappell looked at the Talker and turned on his recorder, wondering what to expect.

"Billy," the Talker repeated.

"I don't like to be called Billy," said Chappell. "Can you call me Bill?"

The Talker quickly responded, "Bill." Pause. "E." Then came a rapid-fire, punctuated, "Billy. Billy. Billy. Billy."

The odd and skin-tingling thing was, Billy is Chappell's legal first name, not William or Bill. Who "out there" knew that? And knew that he did not like to be addressed as Billy? The mystery talker behind the Talker never revealed itself.

Whoever it was liked to spook others, too. Another time, Chappell had a friend (we'll call him Jim pseudonymously) visiting at his home. Jim, who was rather skeptical about spirit communications devices, was playing with the Talker, laughing at it.

"Say my name," said Jim, not expecting an answer.

The Talker spelled out his last name letter by letter.

Jim froze, a look of disbelief on his face. "Tell me it didn't just say that," he said to Chappell.

Before Chappell could respond, the Talker answered, "That's you."

Jim suddenly looked a little pale. He reached down, turned the Talker off, and said, "I don't ever want to see that again."

EXTRATERRESTRIALS AND ALIEN BEINGS

Since the beginnings of high-tech spirit communications over a century ago, researchers have believed themselves to be in contact with extraterrestrials. Tesla gave thought to this, and Marconi wondered about signals from Mars.

Sarah Estep collected approximately two thousand Electronic Voice Phenomena from beings who seemed to be extraterrestrials and not the dead. At first, Estep made the distinction between the two based on the content of their messages. Then she started asking specific questions about other worlds. The ET messages tended to be longer than messages from the dead. All of her ET communications were positive, never dark or threatening. She discovered that other EVP researchers were also getting messages from aliens.

Estep divided ET communications into two categories: hard and soft. The hard communications seemed to come from beings on physical worlds in our universe.

The soft communications seemed to originate in parallel dimensions—perhaps from beings that are versions of ourselves.

The ETs told Estep to tune her television set to Channel 47. Letters appeared on the screen. At first they formed gibberish, and after several days they began spelling out words in English. The first recognizable word was "Venus," repeated many times, followed by "arrived" six days later. Had beings from Venus come to Earth? The answer is not known, but Estep did have some visitations that accompanied her ET Electronic Voice Phenomena.

Estep asked the ET communicators about their god and was told they have different gods. "Our god is with you," they said, and she replied that she was honored that he came.

All of her ET communications were positive, Estep told Rosemary: "I have always felt close to them. They have never been terrible with me. I have had very good contacts with them."

On another occasion, she asked them if they had seasons on their world. They said, "We look like yellow." It was a strange reply, and Estep did not know how to interpret it. The next night, she asked if they meant that the predominant color on their world was yellow, like we would describe our world as predominantly green or blue. A communicator answered, "Say! I say, say not!"

The next morning, Estep was told: "We'll sit, sit by the window." That evening, Estep was sitting in her office reading, with her chair facing the window. Something caused her to look up. She saw a bright yellow light the size of a basketball and the color of the moon float down as though from the sky. It hovered for a few seconds in her window and then vanished. The next day she received the message: "We came down to see you." Had Estep witnessed an intelligent life-form? A couple of decades later, ufologists and paranormal investigators were full of accounts and discussions about "orbs," lights of varying sizes and colors of unknown origins, which often move as though directed by intelligence and in association with UFO activity, the formation of crop circles, and the manifestation of other paranormal phenomena.

Estep believed that she received messages from beings on Venus, Mars, a planet orbiting the star Alpha Centauri, and other places unknown. In addition to leaving messages on her reel-to-reel tape recorder, they implanted thoughts in her head.

Once she was startled to see two beings who looked like human men, dressed in black uniforms and with their backs to her, working on a small box in front of her television set. The vision quickly disappeared, leaving her to wonder if she had imagined it. Later she was told in Electronic Voice Phenomena that the men had come from a craft overhead and had brought black boxes for her office and the television. Estep had the impression that the boxes facilitated communication in English and the appearance of images, words, and symbols on her television screen.

THE PARANORMAL PARROTS

A common phenomenon experienced by many real-time EVP researchers is mimicking, as though the invisible communicators are repeating what they hear. Sometimes the exact or similar words are repeated back, and other times words with the same meaning are said.

After completing tests at Waverly on the same night as the "what-fell communication" mentioned earlier, Chappell and the friend who had tripped made the drive to the man's home in Kentucky. Chappell thought of another experiment. He rolled the passenger window down. "I want you to drive slow, because I'm going to put the Puck on the roof and see what happens," he told his friend. The Puck was quick to comment. "Slowly drive," it said, mimicking Chappell.

Rosemary has encountered the mimics many times. Are the communicators repeating what they hear in order to validate it, or are they being prankish?

At a highly active home in New York State, Rosemary and Phil set up the MiniBox to try to identify the presences who were causing troubling haunting and poltergeist disturbances for the residents who owned the property. Rosemary and Phil identified themselves and the property owner who was present. They began asking questions.

"Can you hear us okay?" Phil asked.

"Okay," a male voice answered.

"Tell us who you are," Phil said.

No answer.

"Tell us who you are," Phil said more emphatically. "Give us your name."

The voice responded, "State your name."

Though they asked repeatedly over the next hour for the communicators to identify themselves, the invisibles refused to do so. Once a voice said, "Dead," in response to, "Who are you?"

Another voice broke in at one point, saying, "You'll have to speak up." So, perhaps it is indeed true that communication is as hard to hear and understand on the other end as it is on our end.

ARE WE TALKING TO OURSELVES IN PARALLEL DIMENSIONS?

The mimicking of communicators has led some researchers to wonder if we are talking to versions of ourselves, either from parallel dimensions or perhaps even time-displaced from the future. "There are times when I think the comments and the way they are structured indicate I might actually be talking to myself," said Chappell.

"Part of the parallel universe theory holds that for everything you do, you create a parallel reality," said Imbrogno. "Some of these realities have only slight differences from the one we are in. For example, there may be a reality where the only difference between you here and you there is, you own a red car instead of a gold one. In other realities, you may be quite different. To me, many of the transmissions don't sound like ghosts, spirits, demons, or extraterrestrials. They sound like people, not here in this world, but somewhere else—maybe a parallel dimension. We could be talking to ourselves, versions of us doing the same thing we are at the same time.

"If all of these other realities exist, they all have different quantum signatures that would make them invisible to us," Imbrogno said. "But you could connect with them through radio waves. If somebody here turns on a Mini-Box and says, 'Hello, is anybody out there?' a near duplicate of that person may be doing the same thing with the same or nearly the same equipment, but in a realm with a different quantum signature. If that 'other' is in a close parallel reality, the oscillators on both boxes will lock into each other."

This may explain why communicators seem to mimic us. It may also explain naming. Many experimenters ask communicators to identify the experimenters who are present by name. Perhaps the communicators name themselves instead of us and we are hearing our own names from versions of ourselves.

These parallel "others" may also be looking to *us* for information and answers at the same time we are hoping that they will enlighten us. Phil and Rosemary had an unusual exchange with communicators at a stone chamber in the Hudson Valley in New York. Phil began researching the mysterious chambers during the Hudson Valley UFO wave in the late 1980s, when he found that UFO sightings corresponded to the locations of chambers.

No one knows who built the chambers or why, but

they appear to be Neolithic in age, possibly done by Celtic explorers. And they are all paranormal hot zones, as Phil and Rosemary have discovered by conducting EVP experiments at them.

The exchange began when Phil's name came over the MiniBox repeatedly: "Phil . . . Phil . . . Philip . . ."

Rosemary said, "Do you have a message for Phil?"

There was a pause and then a voice said flatly, "Not really."

Rosemary and Phil laughed. Was this a Trickster-style joke? they wondered.

On the heels of that another voice broke in, saying, "Rosemary . . . do you have a message . . . for *me*?"

"I absolutely froze," recounted Rosemary. "It doesn't occur to us that we could be the unknown 'aliens' out there to someone else."

It's a complicated picture that can easily make heads spin. The bottom line is, there may be no simple explanation of the identities of the communicators.

TIME DISPLACEMENT

Some Electronic Voice Phenomena may actually be time displacements from our own dimension. Just as people can have clairvoyant visions of the past, called retrocognition, we may have retrohearing as well. One of the most famous examples of retrohearing is the Dieppe air-raid case studied in the early 1950s. The sounds were of a bloody air and sea battle fought on August 19, 1942, during

World War II near Dieppe, France. On August 4, 1951, two Englishwomen visiting near Dieppe heard a replay of the gun- and shell fire, dive-bombing aircraft, and men screaming. The sounds seemed like a real event, but nothing matching the sounds was taking place. Psychical researchers speculated that the women had experienced a spontaneous time displacement.

There's another twist to this as well—we may not tune into the past, per se, but to an ever present, eternal now where everything is happening simultaneously.

Through her research, Rosemary met Misty Dawn, a longtime paranormal experiencer and EVP experimenter. Misty has heard voices that may come from the past. Once Frank Sumption sent her an Electronic Voice Phenomenon he had captured saying, "This is Misty Dawn." Misty was astonished to recognize her own voice—but from a time when she was much younger. "It was a weird, eye-opening experience," she said. "Later on, I got messages about alternate realities and time travel. They made comments about how I am 'here' and 'there' simultaneously. I came to the conclusion that parts of me are in different realities at the same time, including what we call the past."

David Rountree, a researcher in New Jersey with a science and technical background, has documented Electronic Voice Phenomena that seem to be time-shifted. One curious case he investigated involved a Morse code message left as voice mail on a cell phone. The carrier had no record of the call, and it was not transmitted via a cell phone tower. The Morse code indicated an aircraft was about to go down in the Atlantic Ocean east of the Bahamas—but no such accident occurred at the time of the voice mail. Morse code has not been actively used by the military since the 1940s and not by civilian aircraft since the 1950s, nor was it used on the frequency band now used by cell phones, 800MHz. The best explanation is a time displacement anomaly—a residual stray Electronic Voice Phenomenon from the past or perhaps a parallel realm.

PICKING UP THE THOUGHTS OF THE LIVING

For decades, experimenters have recorded voices that seemed to come not from the dead but from the living in this world, both awake and sleeping. Experimenters have heard voices identifying themselves as people the experimenters know who are very much alive—and their voices are recognizable, too. However, the "senders" have no knowledge of the communication. What happens in such a case? We may be picking up something of another person's thoughts or consciousness; if we know them, we may have the right emotional connection to them to enable such a link.

In France, researcher Jacques Blanc-Garin conducted informal experiments in the mid-1990s with sleeping people, who responded in Electronic Voice Phenomena to his questions in a similar fashion to voices believed to be from the dead. Blanc-Garin created ambient noise with the rubbing of paper, German-language conversation, and an air-band receiver.

He asked his sleeping wife if she was present, and she answered, "I am in airs, Poupone" (her nickname for him). Another sleeper was asked to identify an object Blanc-Garin held in his hand; she correctly answered that it was a crystal, implying that her sleeping consciousness had the capability of remote viewing.

Blanc-Garin said he got conclusive results nearly every time. He suggested the process could be useful for people suffering from mental disorders, by using Electronic Voice Phenomena to communicate with the entities or personalities in their thoughts.

Cases such as these raise questions about the identities of EVP communicators. If we cannot relate them to personalities whom we know, then how confident can we be that we are talking to the dead or other spirits? We may be tuning into minds somewhere on the planet—or perhaps in a parallel dimension.

CONNECTIONS TO DEVICES

Some communicators seem to know and respond to the devices used to establish contact. Since starting her research in real-time Electronic Voice Phenomena with ghost boxes, Rosemary has had increasing comments from communicators about the devices themselves. Some of them like the boxes; some of them do not. Those who do not may not appreciate our ability to penetrate into their realm. Perhaps there are those who do not wish us to learn more about them and their worlds.

Other communicators seem drawn to the devices. Once an unknown communicator objected when Rosemary announced the end of a session with a Frank's Box and put the box away in its crate. A raspy, low voice said, "No-o-o-o cra-a-ate . . . no-o-o-o cra-a-ate . . . no-o-o-o cra-a-ate," drawing out the words. Apparently the communicator did not want the session to end.

Researchers who work in EVP grief counseling, who seek contact with specific dead people, have more success with identities, for evidence and voices can be validated by living relatives and friends. When the spirit communications devices are able to maintain better and longer-lasting links, we will be able to make better determinations of identities.

8

The Spiricom Controversy

If you've delved into spirit communications and Electronic Voice Phenomena, you have probably come across the troubled history of Spiricom. The Spiricom was the first widely publicized device that supposedly delivered real-time spirit communications, and with some identifiable communicators. When news of it broke in the 1980s, it was to spirit communications what a UFO on the White House lawn is to ufologists. But the Spiricom was a time bomb of controversy, and when it blew up it rained down shrapnel that still falls all over EVP research today. Were the Spiricom Earth-to-afterlife conversations real, or were they faked? And if they were faked, who was in on it?

Spiricom was birthed in the work of George W. Meek. An engineer by training, unimposing and mild-mannered, Meek believed that technology could deliver reliable real-time, two-way talking with the dead. He believed that proof of the afterlife would transform humanity, and he devoted his postretirement years to that quest. It took Meek and his partners eight years to claim success and put spirit communications on fast-forward.

Author John G. Fuller recorded the story of Spiricom in *The Ghost of 29 Megacycles* (1986). Fuller was approached by Meek to do the book. Meek also wrote about Spiricom himself. The story is glowing, but critics contend that Spiricom was not what it was made out to be. No one has ever been able to prove that Spiricom was faked, and since the principal players, including Fuller, are all dead, the complete truth may never be known. We'll look at both sides of the controversy.

First, the story according to Fuller and Meek.

GEORGE MEEK'S BACKGROUND

After earning his bachelor's degree in engineering in 1932, Meek worked in product development in industry and business and was quite successful due to his creativity and drive. Like many inventors, he believed that he received ideas and inspiration telepathically from the spirit world. He became increasingly interested in the paranormal, and especially the idea that technology could provide a way to talk to the dead. By age fifty-five, he knew this would be his next and last quest in life, and he started salting away money for an early retirement. In five years he saved about half a million dollars, quite an impressive sum of money in those days. In 1970, at age sixty, he left his job and threw himself full-time into metaphysics and the paranormal. For the next twenty years he worked in projects he said that he directed and financed himself.

For Meek, this work entailed the highest spiritual motivations. He wanted to bring together science and religion. This was not just about technology. This involved God, the meaning of life and creation, and the very substance of the universe itself. Meek created his own idea of a meta-science, that is, over and above all fields of science.

Meek's first project involved psychic healing. He went abroad—and paid for medical professionals to do so as well—to study energy healing. He received validation of what he already believed, that this reality teems with unseen energies and most people remain unaware of them. He observed mediums who had healing gifts and learned how most said they were aided by discarnate beings who communicated with them directly through clairvoyance and clairaudience. *What if the same principle could work with discarnate scientists and inventors?* Meek wondered. Could he find a medium who could talk to dead people who had the right technical background to help him establish direct communication between the living and the dead?

Meek founded a research laboratory in Philadelphia "to work exclusively on the project that had foiled Marconi and Edison—a communication system capable of two-way conversation with the higher levels of consciousness," as he put it.

MEEK'S INVOLVEMENT IN ELECTRONIC VOICE PHENOMENA

The evidence of EVP had already convinced Meek that real-time communication was possible. He formed Metascience Associates, a partnership with several like-minded persons. They made mediumistic contact with Dr. Francis G. Swann, a physicist who had died in 1962. Swann assembled a group of dead colleagues from the astral and mental causal planes to give advice and guidance on technology. With that guidance, Meek and his partners built a device called the Mark I, a setup of a tape recorder, oscillators, preamps, transistors, timers, and relays, with a 300MHz generator shielded from radio interference. They engaged the services of a medium and began holding high-tech séances. The men sat around the medium, who attempted to communicate with Swann, while the equipment stood ready to capture any direct communication.

The medium would go into a trance and allow Swann to speak through him. But in session after session, nothing came directly over the equipment. Speaking through the medium, Swann informed the men that the situation was far more complicated than it appeared on the surface and involved more than just sound frequencies. Higher radio frequencies were necessary, as well as the type of diodes used by Raudive for amplifying voices. In addition, Swann said, there would be no success without the "active application of energies" from those on the Other Side. In other words, the dead had to enable the process—it could not be accomplished by the living alone.

Swann later elaborated on what he meant by "application of energies." He and others who were working with him on the Other Side used their powers of mind energies to create voice patterns. Swann said "thought" did not adequately capture everything that these mind energies embody, but the term was close enough. This effort from the dead needed to be combined with Earth-based technology to create audible voices.

The discarnate researchers had no immediate solution to the difficulties, demonstrating that being dead does not automatically endow a person with all-seeing, all-knowing wisdom. Meek and his partners and Swann and his group labored to find the right mix for success. Swann emphasized that the researchers on both sides needed to approach this work with the purpose of joy and helping others, not for selfish gain or glory.

SPIRICOM IS BORN

Spiricom became a series of devices, called the Mark I, Mark II, and so on. The basic device was a modified ham radio transmitting on the AM band. It had a tone generator that created thirteen separate frequencies within the voice range of adult man. The tones were combined into a regular audio carrier, which was broadcast a short distance via a 29MHz AM transmitter (29.575 MHz) to a 29MHz AM receiver. The resulting sound came out a speaker. A cassette recorder for capturing the sessions was placed across the room from the receiver. The entire room served as an echo chamber. The hope was that spirits would use this frequency and the tones as vocal cords for creating words. The room itself was a sort of Faraday cage, shielded from the interference of outside electromagnetic waves. Of all the models created, Mark IV eventually would be the one that worked the best.

Meek became convinced that a medium, preferably a healer, who could produce ectoplasmic materializations like the mediums of the Spiritualist day might be the key to helping him master the subtle forces involved in spirit communications. In 1973 he discovered the man who would give him the breakthrough he sought: an American medium named William (Bill) O'Neil. Meek learned about O'Neil through Henry Nagorka, the editor of *Psychic Observer*, an American Spiritualist publication.

BILL O'NEIL BECOMES INVOLVED

O'Neil, a native Pennsylvanian, had the background that Meek was looking for. Meek wrote O'Neil a letter inviting him to join the experiments of Metascience Associates.

O'Neil seemed to have a natural gift for healing by a laying on of hands, and his professional background involved radio, rocketry, and electronics. He was convinced that he could invent a device that would enable the deaf to hear. He described himself as an artist, poet, and composer. He also was a ventriloquist and worked with children's puppets—something not explored by Fuller in the book, which critics would focus on years later.

Most of the controversy over Spiricom falls on the shoulders of O'Neil, who died in 1992. He did have his problems—profound mood swings and constant financial troubles. Fuller portrayed him as a reluctant prophet who never sought any fame or glory. Rather, he reportedly considered Spiricom an obstacle to some of his other work that he felt called to do. He repeatedly announced he was quitting, only to be talked out of it by Meek.

A few months prior to the arrival of Meek's letter, O'Neil was deep into experimenting with radio frequency oscillators, trying to find the right frequency that would help the deaf hear. One night he had an experience that was so astonishing it frightened him. He was working with two oscillators placed by the sides of his aquarium and was beating their frequencies together. Suddenly he noticed that the water in the fish tank started swirling, forming cloudy shapes and colors. The shapes manifested into human body parts—a hand, an arm, and even part of a head with hair. The beating frequencies seemed to be forming ectoplasm.

O'Neil was so shocked that he doubted his sanity, and he stopped his experiments for two weeks. When he resumed them, the body parts formed again in the water. This time strange energies coursed through O'Neil's body, making him shake violently. Again he stopped his experiments, and he even visited a doctor to determine if there was anything physiologically wrong with him. He was given a clean bill of health.

O'Neil went looking for answers to his bizarre experiences, and he wrote a letter to Nagorka at *Psychic Observer.* Not long after that, Meek's letter arrived.

O'Neil did not leap at the invitation. He told Meek he had no desire to repeat these experiments outside of controlled laboratory conditions. Furthermore, he had no desire to spend the rest of his days in a mental institution. Clearly, he was still worried about effects on his sanity. Meek persisted, patiently writing letters of encouragement.

THE DOC NICK BREAKTHROUGH

Two years later, in 1975, O'Neil had another mind-blowing experience. One night while he was composing music on his guitar—O'Neil believed he received creative inspiration from disembodied sources—an apparition materialized in front of him. It was a man, who spoke clearly in an audible voice, introducing himself as Doc Nick. He said he had been a doctor and a ham radio operator when he was alive and that O'Neil had the potential to become a "really rare and unusual healer" and he would give him guidance for accomplishing that. Then the voice disappeared.

Doc Nick began making more appearances, but only to O'Neil. O'Neil's wife, Mary Alice, could never see or hear him. Doc Nick gave instructions to Bill on how to heal with his hands and also how to build electronic devices that could be used for healing. He had some remarkable successes, included the healing of a woman with lymphosarcoma.

Meek finally persuaded O'Neil to work with him. O'Neil did so reluctantly, still worried about his ability to maintain his mental stability. He insisted on remaining in his rural home near Pittsburgh, Pennsylvania. O'Neil worked on Spiricom at home and communicated with Meek mostly by mail.

O'Neil built a crystal microphone to record Doc Nick's voice but could not capture it. He continued with a clumsier method of repeating onto a tape recorder what he could clairaudiently hear Doc Nick saying, just as a medium repeats unheard spirit messages for clients.

In February 1977, Doc Nick made one of his appearances and told O'Neil that he was now communicating with someone new to him on the Other Side—a Dr. Swann, who was building something. Would O'Neil fill him in?

Meek was excited at this development, but progress stalled again. They tried ultraviolet spirit photography but without success. O'Neil became frustrated to the point of nearly giving up.

GEORGE MUELLER APPEARS

In July 1977, O'Neil had another rallying breakthrough. On the heels of another ultraviolet photography failure, O'Neil went to burn his photographs in his living room fireplace. Just as he was about to throw the first photo into the flames, he felt a hand on his shoulder. Thinking it was his wife, he turned, and was startled to see the figure of a distinguished man dressed in a business suit. It was an apparition. The man said he needed O'Neil's help to carry out some research and he in turn could help O'Neil with his failed research.

The stranger gave O'Neil details about his identity and life that O'Neil could verify by checking records. His name was George Mueller. He had been an electrical engineer and physicist, and he had once worked for the U.S. Signal Corps. O'Neil taped the conversation, but on playback only his lone voice was heard. It sounded as though he were having a one-way conversation.

This still was terrific news to Meek. He investigated Mueller's credentials. Almost everything checked out, including Mueller's Social Security number and death certificate. Walter Uphoff, a friend of Meek's, found an old photograph of Mueller. But Meek was unable to track down one piece of crucial evidence, a booklet Mueller said he wrote on electronics for the U.S. Army. Nonetheless, the evidence was impressive that the apparition was who he said he was. (The booklet was eventually discovered in out-of-print Army literature.)

Despite this advancement, Meek still had to keep O'Neil from jumping ship. The medium complained of poor finances and said he had to give up the Spiricom research to earn money. His healing work was more important. Meek gave him money and agreed to finance research into healing that Doc Nick was guiding. But the Spiricom research was extremely important, Meek told O'Neil, reminding him that it could impact the entire world. If they could capture the voice either of Doc Nick or George Mueller on tape, Meek and O'Neil would prove survival after death.

O'Neil entered into an odd relationship with his two main dead contacts. Doc Nick and Mueller did not seem to know each other or be interested in each other. Independently, they both provided technical advice. Finally, in October 1977, O'Neil got the breakthrough he was searching for. At last he heard a raspy real-time voice that identified itself as belonging to Doc Nick. The dead man's first words were, "All right. Do you hear me now, Bill? Can you hear me, Bill?"

Their recorded conversation went on for about three minutes, with Doc Nick suggesting modifications to the Spiricom frequencies for better reception. Even though O'Neil had been working for a long time toward this history-making moment, he was still so stunned he could hardly speak without a shaky voice.

Doc Nick's technical advice included switching from the white noise preferred by most EVP researchers to audio frequencies. The audio frequencies would serve as an energy source that Doc Nick could use for projecting his "astral" vocal cords. It sounded plausible to Meek, because he and his partners had observed how EVP voices needed to "steal" energy from sound in order to speak. Sounds included radio frequencies, spoken or sung words, music, and white and pink noise.

Meek was ecstatic with the breakthrough—but also

realistic. Despite the recording, he was not about to rush out to the world with it. He recalled all too well the reaction to Edison's invention of the phonograph, when some scientists dismissed it as nothing more than ventriloquism. Credibility was important, and Meek was hopeful that other researchers, such as some in Europe with whom he was in contact, would be able to corroborate his results.

The groundbreaking recorded conversation was followed by a worrisome silence. Doc Nick continued to communicate clairaudiently with O'Neil in his head, but the medium could not recapture Doc Nick's voice on tape. And then he mysteriously vanished, never to return.

O'Neil was greatly discouraged by this setback and once again considered bailing out of Spiricom. He was dealt a severe blow in 1979, when an arsonist set fire to O'Neil's home. Everything in it was lost, including all of his research equipment. Only the shell of the house remained. Somehow O'Neil managed to pick himself up from this disaster, and he vowed to rebuild his house and resume the spirit communications work.

CONVERSATION WITH A DEAD MAN

On September 23, 1980, O'Neil achieved another breakthrough, sustaining a thirteen-minute conversation with Mueller. The voice of the dead man was robotic and zombielike, with a continuous buzzing sound underneath it. It dragged out some of the syllables.

For a first real-time conversation, it was surprisingly

ordinary. There were no grand pronouncements about making history or revealing secrets of life, death, and the afterlife. Instead, the discarnate Mueller gave advice on tuning O'Neil's frequencies. Echoing Edison, he recited part of the nursery rhyme "Mary's Little Lamb." The conversation went like this:

MUELLER: Now, William, did you understand? W-i-l-l–i-i-a-a-m-m?

O'NEIL: Yes sir, I understand, Doctor.

MUELLER: Very well. I will give you a count from one to ten. One. Two. Three, four, five, six, seven, eight, nine, ten. One moment, William.

O'NEIL: Okay.

MUELLER: Very well, then. Mary had a little lamb; the lamb would go-ooo-goooooo. Play that back for me, William. William?

O'NEIL: Yes, sir.

MUELLER: Play that back for me.

O'NEIL: All right, Doctor. I am sorry; I was lighting a cigarette.

MUELLER: Oh, those cigarettes again!

[O'Neil plays back the tape.]

MUELLER: Did you change it [the frequency], William?

O'NEIL: Yes, I did, Doctor.

There followed several more tests of counting numbers while Mueller advised on more frequency changes.

Over an eighteen-month period, Mueller periodically conversed with O'Neil on tape. The dead doctor was a night owl, preferring to chat between two and four in the morning. (Once when O'Neil complained about the hour, Mueller said the medium should know that there was no awareness of time "over here.") The content of the conversations ranged from mundane to technical; Mueller seemed focused on perfecting the ability to communicate. Amazingly, he could see the layout of O'Neil's lab, as well as any magazines or books O'Neil placed out. Sometimes O'Neil laid out articles, which Mueller read and then discussed.

Sometimes the conversations abruptly terminated without warning or explanation, as though a connection had been lost. Meek speculated that solar and electromagnetic activity, as well as other unknown factors, interrupted the link. It was not unlike being booted off the Internet—only O'Neil had little control over reestablishing contact.

Meek's research associates tried their hand at Spiricom, and other spirits besides Mueller came through. But no one had the success that O'Neil did. It would not last, even for O'Neil. After eighteen months and twenty hours of taped conversations, Mueller gave a forewarning: "I cannot be here forever. I cannot guarantee how long I'll be visiting here. Do you understand, William? . . . There is a time and a place for everything. So as I have mentioned before, this is something I think you should be aware of."

Then one day about a month later, Mueller vanished from the scene without farewell. Meek believed that his postmortem energy frequency changed, raising him up to a higher and more remote realm that the Spiricom Mark IV electronics were incapable of registering.

TELLING THE WORLD ABOUT SPIRICOM

It was a blow, but Meek now felt he had what he needed to break the news of proof of the afterlife to the world. In August 1981, he organized a press conference in Washington, D.C. The response of the media was tepid, but a respectable showing of print, radio, and television reporters attended the press conference. Meek played excerpts of the O'Neil-Mueller recordings. He expressed his hope that major research companies like AT&T, IBM, Bell Laboratories, and ITT would get involved.

The journalists were respectful and asked serious questions, but their coverage ranged from nothing at all, to objective reporting, to ridicule. Some of the newspaper headlines were "Dial D for Dead," "New Communications Systems a Grave Matter," and "Reach Out, Reach Out and Haunt Someone." The *Chicago Sun-Times* overdid itself in purple prose, dismissing the tapes as sounding "like Igor responding to Dr. Frankenstein through a closed door on a windy night in Transylvania." Writers joked about calling up famous dead people to ask them silly questions. Fortunately, other journalists presented a straightforward report. Undaunted, Meek gave dozens of radio interviews and kept playing clips from the O'Neil-Mueller recordings.

Meek's hopes for revolutionizing the world and ushering in an age of brotherhood were soon dashed. The evidence failed to move the public, and the corporate world was silent. In order to quell critics, Meek submitted his tapes for tests that proved that Mueller's voice was neither his nor O'Neil's voice. The tests upheld the tapes, but few seemed to care.

In addition, Meek sent out the schematics for Spiricom to hundreds of technicians, but no one could replicate his results. It seemed that all the years Meek and others had invested were about to be drowned in a sea of apathy.

Then Meek received a letter from abroad. It came from a respected scientist who requested anonymity. The scientist told Meek he and others in Europe had been pursuing similar work since 1946. Meek was on the right track, the scientist assured him. He offered the professional expertise of himself and his colleagues to Meek.

Meek's Metascience Associates attracted grant money and funded some of the more promising spirit communications researchers. Meek's results continued to stand alone. Others achieved significant results, but no one duplicated Spiricom.

THE END

In the 1980s, Meek and his wife, Jeanette, moved to North Carolina, where Meek bought a tract of land and developed it as a subdivision. He had dreams of attracting people there to create a spiritually minded community. He conducted many experiments in his home laboratory. Some involved the consciousness of plants, and others concerned ultraviolet spirit photography.

In the 1990s, Meek became involved with European EVP researchers, and then he abruptly retreated into private mediumistic work with his housekeeper, Loree, who was communicating with the dead.

After Spiricom, O'Neil deteriorated. Toward the end of his life, he was diagnosed with schizophrenia and was confined to the Torrance State Hospital in Derry Township, Pennsylvania. He died there in 1992. Sarah Estep was aware of his condition but had promised Meek she would never mention it until after both O'Neil and Meek were dead. Was Meek trying to cover it up?

Meek never waivered in his support of O'Neil. In a memorial he composed for O'Neil, he invoked Marconi and Edison:

During the 17 years that I was privileged to know and work with Bill, I developed a tremendous admiration for his knowledge in the field of electronics—particularly the fields of radio and television. I soon found that his basic knowledge was supplemented by an intuitive-psychic ability that fully deserved the term paranormal. Merely by touching a radio or TV set, he often instinctively knew where the defect or breakdown had developed.

Bill's psychic abilities of seeing and communicating with persons dwelling in the spirit worlds ranked with the best such talents I uncovered in a worldwide search. The combination of those capabilities with his electronic skills enabled him to succeed on a project which had eluded the efforts of Edison and Marconi.

In 1980–82, Bill became the first person in the history of Mankind to log more than 20 hours of meaningful two-way communication with persons who no longer lived in their physical bodies. By freely sharing the results of his efforts with younger people the world over, researchers in many countries have carried the work further and have provided solid evidence that each person's mind, memory banks, personality and soul transcend death of the physical body.

Meek quoted another EVP researcher, Bill Weisensale, who said that "O'Neil was such a strong psychic, he could probably communicate with the Spirit Worlds using two tin cans and a piece of string."

O'Neil reportedly communicated with Loree, talking about the multiple entities that had been inside him and how they had been responsible for the cancer that destroyed him, ending his life twenty years too soon. He also commented on his fondness for ventriloquism and that he had learned that he would be able to use it in working with children in the Beyond. In one message to Meek, O'Neil said he no longer had "those split personalities," and said he was sorry "that I let the other entities take me over."

Meek died in 1999, without seeing the day he envisioned, that people the world over would realize that death is not final and would start to live better, more spiritual lives. Those hopes continue to be nurtured by others who have followed in Meek's footsteps.

Now let's take a look at what some of the critics have to say.

WAS SPIRICOM A HOAX OR A GENTLE DECEPTION?

As early as 1987, doubts were being raised about the authenticity of Spiricom, or "Spiricon," as some dubbed it. In the ensuing years, experimenters have examined Spiricom and tried to duplicate its success. No one seems to have attained Mueller-like conversations, but some have successfully used Meek's tones to obtain Electronic Voice Phenomena.

Alexander MacRae, a leading spirit communications researcher from Scotland, had doubts about Spiricom early on. When news of Spiricom broke after the press conference, MacRae wanted to find out more, not only because of his EVP research but also because his father had recently died and he thought perhaps Spiricom might be a way to have live contact with him. In 1982 MacRae sent away for information and received leaflets offering a Spiricom for ten thousand dollars, which he thought was rather pricey. Then Meek sent him a copy of the real system and it seemed evident to MacRae that the ten-thousand-dollar price was to cover research and development costs. However, the system was no mystical machine. "The heart of it was a little radio bug of the sort available from electronic hobbyists' shops for a couple of dollars," he said. After some study, MacRae concluded that there was "no way" that Spiricom would produce the results claimed.

MacRae wanted to see Spiricom in action and in 1982 undertook a trip to Meek's home in Franklin, North Carolina. He flew to Atlanta and waited in a motel for Meek's permission to come to Franklin. Instead, MacRae got a string of reasons why a visit would not be possible. Eventually he left Atlanta, did some traveling in the United States, and then again contacted Meek before returning to England. MacRae never got to see Spiricom. All of the reasons given by Meek were plausible, MacRae said, but the whole situation just did not add up.

There were a number of things about Spiricom that unsettled MacRae over the course of time, among them:

- No voices came over Spiricom after December 1981, so no one was able to see live a demonstration after the worldwide publicity event.
- There was no good explanation why all communicators disappeared.
- Mueller showed little knowledge of electronics in his technical advice to O'Neil.
- The actual sources of all of Meek's research funds were not fully accounted for.
- In 1982 Meek sent MacRae a tape with the Spiricom noise to use as a sound source, which

MacRae used with his own equipment; it did not produce voices.

- A psychologist in Mendocino, California, Wilson van Deusen, had conducted research trying to communicate with voices heard by mental patients and had noted that Fred and Doc were two common names of alleged spirits cited by the patients. O'Neil had two "docs" and another favorite spirit communicator named Fred Engstrom, who said he had been a farmer in rural Virginia and died in 1830.

In 1983 the Meeks visited MacRae at his home and laboratory on the Isle of Skye in Scotland. MacRae told him of his doubts about Spiricom, but Meek said he believed the results to be true. He said he had witnessed O'Neil working Spiricom and had made a video of a session. Meek admitted that O'Neil had insisted on being filmed with his back to the camera, which MacRae found odd. He wondered if O'Neil was concealing a type of electrolarynx, a tube to inject noise into his mouth so that he could create Mueller's voice. Meek said he would let MacRae see the video, but he never made it or a copy available.

Twenty years later, in 2003, MacRae finally saw the video televised in a documentary. The video reinforced MacRae's thought that O'Neil had done the speaking for Mueller by having noise injected into his mouth. At no time did O'Neil and Mueller ever overlap each other in speech. MacRae also felt that O'Neil's body language gave him away, even with his back turned to the camera. He used the same dramatic upper body movements while both he and Mueller were speaking. When people listen to another talking, they do not gesticulate as they do when they are speaking themselves.

MacRae's final assessment of Spiricom was not favorable. He said it amounted to a betrayal of serious experimenters for the sake of personal prestige.

O'Neil was in possession of an electrolarynx at the time of his death, and some skeptics believe that he used it to alter his voice to speak as the spirit communicators. The electrolarynx is in the Spiricom archives now held by Thomas Pratt, the president of the Metascience Foundation, in Orlando, Florida.

MacRae was not the only expert in Electronic Voice Phenomena to have trouble with Spiricom. In 2002 Sarah Estep wrote an open letter about her experiences. She said that Meek contacted her and asked her to experiment with Spiricom herself. O'Neil had been the only person to use the system, and Meek wanted to see if someone else could obtain the same results. Estep had an impressive EVP track record.

Estep agreed, and Meek arrived with Spiricom and set it up in her home. Estep did not say if this was the original device used by O'Neil or a copy. Whatever it was, it was much smaller than the setup portrayed with O'Neil in photographs. She agreed to use the Spiricom sounds only, and she signed a nondisclosure agreement.

Estep put the Spiricom tones on an endless loop tape and made five-minute recordings. She had high anticipation of two-way conversations, but none manifested in a month of recordings. She heard voices, almost as good as the ones she got on her air-band radio system, but none of them sounded like the O'Neil recordings. The voices answered her questions but in standard Electronic Voice Phenomena, not real-time, two-way.

Meek called Estep weekly to check on her progress. He said he had asked O'Neil to ask Mueller to contact her, and Mueller said he would—but O'Neil said he had to give him "directions" on how to find where Estep was living. Said Estep:

> Guess the directions weren't too good, for I never heard from Mueller.
>
> I was very disappointed, that I wasn't having anything like O'Neil. My contacts were very good, but they (as I said) had not changed. I wanted to have long 2-way conversations (with Mueller) if possible, or at least with someone else. I told George this, each time he called. He was very kind and patient about my feelings (although I'm sure he was terribly disappointed) since my results were still the same. After a month I told George, I really didn't want to continue with Spiricom. I used it for 30 days, never missing a one, and wasn't having the kind of contacts O'Neil had.

One of the more recent efforts to duplicate Spiricom was done by Craig Telesha, of Mechanicsburg, Pennsylvania, one of the leading tech experts in paranormal investigation. Telesha acknowledged that it would be easy to debunk Spiricom as a "glorified walkie-talkie system." There would be no need for an elaborate hoax of electrolarynxes and ventriloquism, for the amateur radio band could have been used as the medium for short-range communication.

Telesha obtained the schematics and attempted to re-create the original 29MHz device. Thanks to advances in radio circuitry and technology, his Spiricom was much smaller than O'Neil's setup, using a walkie-talkie transmitter and receiver pair, which were retuned up from 27 MHz to 29.575 MHz. The transmitter portion was a microprocessor that created the thirteen original mixed tones. The units were placed about ten feet apart. Telesha and others who have used this device report good results with standard Electronic Voice Phenomena—but no real-time, two-way conversations similar to Spiricom.

Dr. Stephen Rorke (a professor who has lectured on developmental psychology, cognition, theoretical and applied physics) undertook a comprehensive investigation of the Spiricom evidence from 2003–2009 and concluded that the two-way conversations were not genuine. While certain the evidence was hoaxed by ventriloquist O'Neil using an electrolarynx device held in proximity of his mouth, Rorke noted, there remains the possibility the hoax was a product of O'Neil's schizophrenic mental condition combined with Meek's desire to believe. In other

words, both might have genuinely believed that true results had been obtained. The situation may have been
comparable to "the same psychological dynamic that can
take place at a Ouija board session where there is nothing
paranormal going on, but each person convinces the other
that something is," said Rorke.

Rorke traveled to Florida to meet with Thomas Pratt
(President of Metascience Foundation), and on January 1,
2009, visited the hangar where Pratt was storing the Spiricom technology, recordings, and all primary source docu-
ments related to the strange case of Spiricom. Rorke, who
was allowed unfettered access to all the materials, found
the Spiricom components in a state of disrepair, and connected the functional components to no avail. Pratt has
since begun restoration of the technology.

Even if Spiricom was faked, it does not discredit EVP
as a whole, Rorke said. "EVP has such an expansive data
set, it seems unlikely it has been hoaxed by everyone, even
if there are fraudulent data points within the set," he said.
EVP is worthy of scientific study, and may actually be
"perinormal" ("in the vicinity of" normal), rather than paranormal, and thus phenomena outside the standard model
of physics. Rorke, who advocates that "the role of science
should be to investigate the unexplained, not explain the
uninvestigated," promotes a "best evidence standards" approach to evaluating EVP in order to determine the authenticity of the phenomena and the potential implications for
further study EVP has for physics and psychology.

The evidence against Spiricom, as convincing as it is to

some, is still circumstantial. With all of the principal players gone, their supporters and detractors are left to build their cases. Supporters of Spiricom contend that the device worked for O'Neil because of his mediumistic abilities and so it was unique to him. Researchers, including MacRae, have indeed found mediumistic ability to be a key to success in spirit communications. Time and time again, some researchers get results that others do not, even when using the same or similar equipment and following the same or similar procedures—which often makes validating results difficult.

We may never know what really happened behind the scenes at Spiricom. However, it remains one of the most important episodes in the history of modern spirit communications. True or false, Spiricom galvanized countless other researchers around the world.

9

Enter the Ethereals

Whether he realized it or not, Meek influenced researchers everywhere, including some Europeans who in turn ushered in a new set of spirit communicators: the ethereals.

Inspired by Spiricom, Jules Harsch and Maggy Harsch-Fischbach of Luxembourg and Ernst Senkowski of Germany developed a new field that Senkowski, a physicist and professor of engineering, christened "instrumental transcommunication." It involved the recorder, radio, telephone, fax, computer, and television. Technology, they believed, would replace humans as the interface to the spirit world.

Instrumental Transcommunication or ITC, promised

an exciting era. Maggy and Jules, at the center of this new universe, became convinced that "God and Science" could and should work together. Like Meek, they envisioned revolutionizing the world with proof of the afterlife.

Maggy and Jules did not want to be just moderately successful; they wanted to establish groundbreaking research. By the end of 1985 they had a small group of four in Luxembourg, which they called the Cercle d'Etudes sur la Transcommunication de–Luxembourg (CETL). They met once a week for recording sessions via radio and microphone. The voices that came through were typical of Electronic Voice Phenomena: some were loud and clear; others were faint and distorted. Maggy and Jules kept quiet, however, wanting to build a body of evidence before going public with their results.

They named their communications setup the Eurosignal Bridge (ESB). It included two FM radios tuned near 87MHz, a black-and-white television set tuned to a free channel, a Koenig's generator, two ultraviolet lamps, and a loudspeaker with a filter. The audio signal of the television was passed through a parametric filter into an audio amplifier and drove a CB filter and loudspeaker combination. A fluorescent lamp and an incandescent blinking lamp with a one-second rate helped to establish rhythmic timing for the production of speech. Maggy and Jules used a handheld microphone to record the spirits' speech. For reasons they did not explain, Maggy and Jules were told to point flashlights at each FM radio during a session.

The group sent out a regular invitation to the deceased Konstantin Raudive to come through, but several months went by without results. Then, in the spring of 1986, a clear male voice boomed, "Here it is summer, always summer!" It sounded like Raudive. The researchers were elated.

The communications began to flow more easily. In April 1986 they heard their first spirit voices over the television set, but without any images. Raudive began to deliver lengthy lectures. Most of the contacts lasted from ten to fifteen minutes, obtained between 87 and 92MHz. The voices usually came through one of the radio receivers but sometimes emanated from the television set.

COMMUNICATORS FROM HIGHER REALMS
AND PARALLEL WORLDS

Then a change happened. Another communicator, who spoke in a high-pitched, computer-like voice, started making regular appearances. This entity, who seemed like a "he," lectured in an authoritative manner on a wide range of technical and esoteric subjects, as well as history, science, mathematics, and religion. He knew a lot about the goings-on of Earth. Soon this entity was opening and closing every session.

Asked for his name, the communicator astonished the group by giving no ordinary earthly name. In fact, he wasn't even human. Nor had he ever been in a physical form. He said he could be called "Technician," a name that described his function rather than him personally. Technician said he was a member of "The Seven," a council of ethereals, to whom names are not important. Technician said he was assigned to Earth and he (as well as others in the spirit realm) could influence people by impressing information into their consciousness.

More information came forth about The Seven, who began communicating with other researchers as well. They said they were part of the "Rainbow People," a race of higher beings almost beyond the comprehension of humans. They existed in realms of timelessness and spacelessness and were assigned to help the Earth. They had to lower their vibration just to get to the astral plane—the afterlife region—in order to communicate, and when they did so they shimmered in rainbow colors.

The Seven said they were genderless and were not any form of life known to humans. Nor were they angels, ascended masters, or "light beings." However, they were like angels in that they were close to God. They had great wisdom and goodness, and their entire being was illuminated by understanding and forgiveness. They were described by the dead who encountered them as brilliant beings like "banks of supercomputers exchanging oceans of information at lightning speed."

The Seven each had their own individual natures but existed as a group fused together. They served as a "Gatekeeper between Heaven and Earth, between time and space." They had stayed in this assignment for eons, providing assistance, guidance, and support to people on Earth.

They compared their role to a popular Victorian print of an angel guiding two children across a bridge—except they had no wings. They have been particularly active with the Earth during critical periods of history. There have been six such crisis points in the past, and the Earth was now in a seventh critical period and they were trying to awaken humanity to a higher level of consciousness to be prepared for the "End Time."

Technician said the Rainbow People were attracted to Maggy because of her sincerity and interest and had chosen her to assist them in their efforts to build a communications bridge to Earth. She would be aided by Timestream, a "trans team" of deceased scientists, relatives, technical experts, celebrities, and others who now lived on the astral plane in a world called Marduk, similar to Earth but with three suns. The ultimate goal would be to establish receiving stations around the world. Technician's role was to help build this network with other ethereals and the dead, and he began providing technical information for the creation of an Instrumental Transcommunication receiving station on Earth. The Timestream sending station in the astral plane would be operated by Swejen Salter, a deceased female scientist from one of Earth's parallel dimensions.

According to Salter, she once lived on a physical planet named Varid, where she worked as a physicist. She became involved in experiments that produced an anti-energy intended to nullify atomic energy to counter the drifting apart of the universe. The anti-energy was released into a sealed laboratory for testing, with the intent that it would then be released into the atmosphere of the planet. But the anti-energy had a horrifying effect: it reversed the aging process. Most people would find that quite welcome, but this process had no end or limits: everyone exposed to the anti-energy would regress to the point of premature infancy and die. The scientists locked the lab and attempted to destroy the anti-energy, but a great explosion happened, and Salter, thirty-eight, was killed. At the time of her first contact with the Europeans, she had been in the afterlife only two months, on the third level of the astral plane.

As for her death, Salter said she had been unprepared for dying and did not remember her transition. She awakened on a recliner in a "cheerfully decorated" room that was unfamiliar to her. As soon as she was awake, a tall man came in and introduced himself as Sir Richard Francis Burton, the intrepid British explorer who had discovered Lake Tanganyika in Africa in the nineteenth century. Burton died in 1890. He offered to show Salter around in her new world, and she became his companion, working with him in Instrumental Transcommunication.

Salter said she did not miss Varid but at first had difficulty adjusting to the afterlife, even though everyone she met was friendly and helpful.

NEW TYPES OF CONTACT

With the help of Salter, Technician, Burton, Raudive, and others in Timestream, the Harsch-Fischbach home became the first fully functioning Instrumental Transcommunication receiving station on Earth. As their work progressed, the Harsch-Fischbach couple received numerous other-worldly phone calls and long and clear messages through their radios. Most of the phone calls came from Raudive, who delivered lengthy messages. Raudive said that in order for spirit communications to develop on Earth humans would have to come together in a unified mind of harmony and cooperation.

The ESB provided mostly one-way communication, like traditional Electronic Voice Phenomena. By August 1986, Maggy and Jules had a new setup, called the "Gegensprechanlage" or "GA1," that enabled two-way communication for a few minutes. The GA1 consisted of a radio with a built-in antenna, a shortwave radio placed in a separate room, two diode circuits with special antennas, a "frequency translator circuit" with a built-in microphone, and a small fluorescent lamp.

The first voice to come across the new device was, predictably, that of Raudive, who announced, "This is Konstantin Raudive; soon it will work everywhere!" The GA1 produced better communications, but Technician advised Maggy and Jules to use it only when he instructed, otherwise they would find themselves waking up in a parallel dimension. Did that mean that simply engaging in spirit communications work could literally shoot people off into a parallel world? If so, how would they get back? These and other questions were never really answered.

Technician was soon overseeing all of CETL's communications. He seemed to be able to shore up weak energy in the link and to enable contacts with specific dead people whom the experimenters requested.

Toward the end of 1986, Timestream gave CETL instructions for conducting a video experiment. The images transmitted over the next months showed the recognizable dead and scenes from the astral plane that looked very Earth-like. Technician himself appeared in a blurry image. Terms such as "the dead" were joined by "transentities," "extraterrestrians," and "ethereals" to describe otherworldly entities.

Excited about their results and convinced that the public would appreciate evidence of the afterlife, Maggy and Jules organized public demonstrations and lectures. Like Meek, they were ridiculed, criticized, and dismissed. Wounded, they pulled back.

However, their unusual work did catch the interest of others who wanted to join the research. Soon other researchers were being contacted by other spirit groups: Lifeline, Centrale, Transgroup Albert Einstein (so-named because the dead scientist was said to be at the helm of it), and ABX Juno, a "group" entity. The *A* stood for "Aussen" (German for external or outside); the *B* stood for "biological," in terms of penetrating earthly biological life-forms, and "X" stood for experiment. Juno was the name of the main communicator. And so it went, like a cornucopia of entities from a *Star Wars* film.

The new spirit communicators were dazzling. They implanted messages and images on computers, left messages on phone answering machines, and put images on television screens. They lectured on science, including astronomy, physics, and biology.

Live images of the astral world showed Earth-like scenes: mountains, forests, buildings, and a couple holding hands and walking out into a lake or ocean. The spirits said that the astral plane afterlife was an idealized mirror of Earth.

The ethereals urged the formation of an international cooperative research effort that would be comparable to an interdimensional United Nations. However, it would succeed only with the right intentions of sincerity, harmony, ethics, and morals; ego and profit could not be factors. At first, an international cooperative effort looked promising.

INSTRUMENTAL TRANSCOMMUNICATION COMES TO NORTH AMERICA

Meek and the European research attracted an American who would become a major figure himself: Mark Macy. In 1988 colon cancer forced him to reevaluate his life. He had been both an agnostic and atheist and was not particularly interested in the paranormal. His confrontation with mortality caused him to make a serious reevaluation of many things. Determined to heal, he became a strict vegetarian and engaged in alternative therapies for body, mind, and spirit. More and more, he contemplated survival after death and the afterlife. Unusual dreams filled his mind at night. In them Macy found himself in laboratories where boxes on tables had tubes of light streaming from them. If he touched a table, his hand stuck to it as though magnetized. Voices whispered to him about what he was seeing and experiencing. Macy's Instrumental Transcommunication education had begun.

In 1991 Macy met Meek at a conference. By that time, Meek had turned over Metascience to Tom Pratt and was working on a series of books on spirit communications that he called *The Property*. Meek also had a foundation, Continuing Life Foundation, Inc., that he wanted someone else to take over so that he could devote himself full-time to the books. Macy, who had experience as a journalist, author, and publisher, seemed like the ideal candidate. Meek still believed that reliable spirit communications equipment could be developed.

Macy was not much interested in short, cryptic EVP messages—what he called "tiny voices on tape." The longer, clear, and real-time messages and images definitely grabbed his attention.

Eager to cut to the big chase, Macy nonetheless was advised by experts to start his involvement in the field with regular Electronic Voice Phenomena, the "tiny voices on tape." He complied and spent several months experimenting with radios tuned to different frequencies, without success, until at last he got a response. He asked, "Can you tell me about any breakthroughs?" and was answered in the unmistakable voice of Raudive, who said, "Your mind's too much in a turmoil." Macy interpreted the answer as advice for how to progress: he had to clear his mind and focus his thoughts.

Eventually, Macy went to Europe and made contact with the CETL group and others. The trip gave him a clear vision of his new destiny. He decided to devote himself full-time to Instrumental Transcommunication.

The years from about 1985 to 1992 were heady ones, full of enthusiasm, cooperation, and excitement. There was much anticipation among researchers that significant breakthroughs were being made that would awe the world and that even bigger ones lay ahead. The days of global cooperation were numbered, however.

UNRAVELING

International cooperation was difficult to put into effect. Friction existed from the beginning, with a soap opera of all-too-human problems: disagreements, ego bruising, skepticism, jealousy, money problems, legal issues, and so on. Despite many good intentions and meetings, researchers disagreed over protocols, the analyses of results, what to disclose to the public, and how. Everyone had their own recipe for success and their own ideas about how to conduct research. Some wanted to keep their work private while others wanted to make it public.

Serious rifts developed among researchers, and skeptics voiced doubts about fraud. The "unified minds" of harmony and cooperation, stressed by the ethereals and other communicators as necessary to the success of the communication bridges, never really got off the ground.

In October 1995, Maggy, Jules, Macy, and twelve others created the International Network for Instrumental Transcommunication (INIT). Headquarters were in Luxembourg with Maggy and Jules; Macy spearheaded a North American division. Membership doubled in INIT's first two years, but problems continued. In 1996 Macy and Meek parted ways. INIT splintered. Macy formed his own group, World ITC, in 1998. By 1999–2000 INIT was finished, and most of the researchers went their separate ways or formed new coalitions.

Rosemary began doing her own EVP experiments with a tape recorder in the 1980s, after reading about Jürgenson and Raudive. Electronic Voice Phenomena have been a part of her ongoing work and investigations into the unknown. She joined INIT in the 1990s and became involved in real-time Electronic Voice Phenomena in 2006. Like many researchers, she prefers an independent path.

THE CLOSING AND OPENING OF DOORS

After Meek died on January 5, 1999, Macy received an EVP message from him saying, "Good luck!" It marked the end of an era in EVP/Instrumental Transcommunication research. Ahead were new directions, solitary paths, new partnerships, and new researchers with new ideas.

Today there are a variety of organizations around the globe that are devoted to Instrumental Transcommunication and spirit communications; an estimated twenty thousand people worldwide conduct various types of research. For the most part, researchers work independently or in small or regional groups, sharing and collaborating as they wish. Researchers have their own teams and guides on the Other Side.

Timestream is still active and has been in contact with Anabela Cardoso, the Portuguese consul general in Vigo, Spain, and the founder of the *ITC Journal*. Cardoso, Spain's ranking woman diplomat, began, like many, as a skeptic. She started experimenting with traditional Electronic Voice Phenomena, holding that if they had any validity, they might help comfort a friend whose young son had died in a sailing accident. After several weeks of sessions, Cardoso obtained what seemed to be a message from the son. Other communicators appeared and advised Cardoso to switch from Electronic Voice Phenomena to direct voices over the radio. She did and began to carry on conversations with spirit communicators.

Macy tried without success to put together other local and international Instrumental Transcommunication groups and then went on to pursue his own path. In dreams and out-of-body meditations, he was taken to Timestream to be shown equipment and to learn about the bridging processes. Too much emphasis just on the technology would not produce success, he was told. The living had to open their hearts to their colleagues on the Other Side for a true collaboration of *spirit*. Macy was determined to foster the needed atmosphere of love as much as possible.

"My main focus now is getting the word out about what we have learned about Instrumental Transcommunication and about humanity through Instrumental Transcommunication, and the paradise destiny that awaits us if we do the right things on Earth with our thoughts and activities," Macy told us. He disseminates information about "The Project."

According to ethereals, humans are a crossbreed of primitive men on Earth and godlike superhumans of Eden, otherwise known as Marduk, a planet that once orbited between Mars and Jupiter. The inhabitants of Marduk blew up the planet with misuse of their technologies. Its marooned colonists went to Earth, where they established Atlantis and crossbred with the primitive natives. Atlantis became a supercivilization that met the same fate as Marduk, destroying itself with its own misused technology. The survivors are the present-day human race. The Seven then came to Earth to help the survivors regain their spiritual birthright through The Project.

The Project, or Project Sothis as it is also called, actually began before the destruction of Atlantis and involved the opening of nonphysical portals to other dimensions, not just for the purpose of communication but also to travel back and forth between the Earth and more subtle realms. The Project was nearly lost in the fall of Atlantis.

Macy was told by ethereals that six attempts at The

Project have been undertaken since post-Atlantean times and all have failed due to human failings. Humans constantly struggle with their animal, or savage, side. The ethereals seek to help humans conquer their savage side and raise their noble side, or spiritual awareness.

The seventh attempt at The Project began with the Earth-based initiative into Instrumental Transcommunication research in the twentieth century. If this attempt does not succeed, according to the ethereals, they may abandon The Project altogether or at least pull back for a while. They desire all of humanity to participate in it, not just one or two cultures. Macy has worked to spread the word about The Project and ways humanity can recover its noble nature.

"That's the crux of the challenge that faces Instrumental Transcommunication today," Macy said. "People need to learn to bring out their noble side and put their savage side on the back burner. That's what it takes to establish a resonant group for a contact field for higher beings to open up long-lasting communication channels. But once animosities and resentments creep into a group, the contact field becomes cloudy and the contacts close down."

Much of the current interest in Instrumental Transcommunication falls into two areas: the popular fascination with the thrill of ghost hunting and, at the opposite end, research into survival after death. For Macy, life after death is not a question but a certainty. Rather than looking for thrills or shreds of survival evidence, we would better serve ourselves by investing time in establishing a communications bridge with finer spirits and starting to communicate with meaningful dialogues. "That is a relationship across dimensions that is built on love and caring for the people on the other side," Macy said. "They feel the same way about us. Making that effort gradually builds more and more potential for great contacts to happen."

QUESTIONS ABOUT IDENTITIES

Some curious questions remain about the identities of the ethereal and the dead. Skeptics of spirit communications like to criticize the presence of the famous dead, contending that such luminaries, if they did indeed exist in the afterlife, would not be communicating with "ordinary" people on this side of the veil. However, the flip argument is used by skeptics as well. If post-death communication is possible, the skeptics argue, then why don't we hear from famous people who have something important to tell us? It's a no-win situation.

For some, the purported contacts with entities like Technician and Swejen Salter have seemed too much like science fiction. Indeed, some unsettling questions arose even in the 1980s about who they really were.

Rémy Chauvin, a French biologist who was also interested in spirit communications, reported in his best-selling book in France, *The Dead Speak to Us* (1994), that in October 1988, Ernst Senkowski came across a book titled *Dialog with the Beyond* by K. H. Jackel, published in Germany in 1984. Some parts of the book were channeled by a medium, Peter von Egloffstein, who communicated with an entity known as "Rabbi Elysee." Said Chauvin: "A good portion of Rabbi Elysee's paragraphs were almost word-for-word like some of those communicated [later] by the Technician."

Chauvin also noted a similar case with the entity Swejen Salter about her life in the afterlife. She said she had a laboratory on the banks of the River of Eternity on the astral planet Marduk and shared a house with the deceased English explorer Sir Richard Burton. Salter said that Marduk was as big as Saturn and the River of Eternity was the only river on the planet. It was thousands of miles long and resembled the river Oceanus mentioned in Greek mythology, which was said to encircle the Earth. Salter said some 60 million dead people lived in camps along the river and they all had "stabilized" in appearance at about age thirty.

Elements of this story, minus Salter, were already in print—in a 1970 science-fiction novel written by Philip José Farmer, titled *Riverworld*.

Had the Harsch-Fischbach couple obtained the Chauvin and Farmer books? If so, was there an inadvertent projection of some sort that "created" Salter and Technician? Was there a hoax? Chauvin was convinced that Maggy and Jules knew nothing of the other sources and heard the information for the first time from the personalities of Salter and Technician. Salter offered up her own explanation: Farmer "must have been inspired when he wrote *The People of the River*."

Chauvin opined that Salter was confused about where she was and imagined herself to be involved in something undertaken by someone else. Another explanation was that her story was her own dream.

Yet another explanation that we should consider, and which may explain the confusing overlaps, is that of parallel worlds. Thus, it is possible and plausible that Salter and Technician are who they say they are—*and* there are other personalities in other worlds saying and experiencing the same or nearly the same things. Their realities may be picked up as inspirations by writers and artists. It is conceivable that Chauvin's medium or an artist such as Farmer could tap into one of these parallel worlds. In Farmer's case, he might have thought it to be a product of his imagination, rather than his mind contacting an alternate reality.

In such a scenario of parallel worlds, it is impossible to say that one world cannot exist because another one nearly identical to it does. As research into both parallel worlds and spirit communications deepens, we are increasingly going to be confronted by such complex and seemingly paradoxical possibilities. There will be few easy, black-and-white answers.

The Harsch-Fischbach couple gave much consideration to their spirit contact experiences and accepted the self-identifications unless someone could prove otherwise. Many other researchers find themselves in the same situation.

10

Life and Sex in the Afterlife

Everyone wants to know what the afterlife is really like. We are taught what to believe, but nothing compares to a firsthand experience. We'll find out when we leave our earthly life, of course, but most of us want to know ahead of time what to expect. We haven't achieved the day yet when we can just cruise on over for a tour on demand and then come back. Many of my *Coast to Coast* listeners, however, do have afterlife experiences in the form of compelling dreams, visions, and near-death experiences. I'm always fascinated by their stories, because I want to know, too, what awaits us on the Other Side.

"I know what the afterlife is like," a woman caller asserted one night on the show. "I've seen it. I had a near-death experience a few years ago when I was on the operating table. I suddenly was in another place that was far away, and I was looking into this most beautiful park. I can't even tell you how beautiful it was—it wasn't like anything I have ever seen before. I could see people there, too. But I couldn't go in—there seemed to be a boundary I couldn't cross. A voice told me I had to go back, it wasn't my time. I wanted to stay—I felt so good. Then all of a sudden I felt myself rushing backward, and then I woke up in the recovery room. They told me later that I had actually died for a few moments on the table."

Most of the testimonies about visions of the afterlife are like that, about happy, alluring places full of beautiful, lush scenery and populated by our departed loved ones, who come forward to welcome us to our new life. The landscapes and colors are brighter and more beautiful than anything found on Earth, even beyond description.

No matter what we think about surviving death, a visit to the afterlife proves to many people that we really don't die. We just move from one world into another.

One night on the topic of the afterlife, a woman called in with her own experience. "Five months after my sister passed on, I was lying awake in bed reading," she said. "All of a sudden, as though someone threw a switch, my eyes got heavy like they weighed fifty pounds apiece. I laid down and turned out the light. Within a few seconds I was out of my body and I could see it. Then someone took my left hand, and it felt like flesh. It was my sister. I said, 'Sherry, it's you!' She said, 'Of course!'

"We went to a place where there were a lot of people. There was an alabaster gazebo. I said, 'Are we dead?'

"She said, 'No, nobody is dead.' She wanted me to tell everyone in the family that she was okay.

" 'Can they see me?' I asked about the people I saw around us.

" 'If they want to,' she said.

"It wasn't a dream, George. I am telling you, I know the difference between something real and a dream. This was *real*."

"I believe you," I told her.

The dark side of the afterlife also exists, people testify. Another *Coast to Coast* caller said he visited the afterlife in a lucid dream. He described it as an imprisoning rectangular tube full of people screaming and crying at being stuck there for eternity. There were no whip-wielding demons, but the place was just as terrifying as traditional hell and the scene shook this man up for quite some time.

Do we create our own heaven or hell out of our beliefs? What do the people who have died have to say? Descriptions of the afterlife have been remarkably similar throughout history, whether they come through dreams and visions, near-death experiences, mediumistic communications, or Electronic Voice Phenomena. Some accounts conform to religious beliefs, but most paint a picture of the afterlife as a continuation of life on Earth, but better—at least in the early stages.

PERPETUAL SUMMER

Back in 1986, the dead Konstantin Raudive described the afterlife as follows: "Here it is summer, always summer." In just a few words, he conjured up visions of the afterlife as a balmy, verdant landscape where everything is in full bloom and life is pleasant. Is that what the afterlife is like—a state of being that mirrors Earth at its most enjoyable?

Human beings have conceived details of the afterlife since biblical times, based on visions, out-of-body experiences, near-death experiences, the teaching of religions, sages, and prophets, and the testimonies of the dead delivered through mediums, channelers, and technology. Fundamentally, most people seem to agree that there is an afterlife, that good people go to a pleasant place, and that bad people go to an unpleasant place. After that, there are many scenarios for what allegedly takes place in the afterlife.

For the most part, the dead tell us that the afterlife is far more fluid and appealing than portrayals taught in religion. For example, Christianity holds that there is a divine judgment and a soul is assigned to either heaven or hell. Heaven is a lofty place of eternal rest in the presence of God and Jesus, surrounded by the company of angels. Hell is a lower realm of eternal punishment ruled by Satan and demons, who inflict unending tortures upon the sinners. The judgment is final; there is no redemption for the damned. Both heaven and hell are forever. Life is a test for stakes in eternity.

The dead tell us a different story: There are rewards for the good and punishments for the wicked, but nothing is eternal. We always have the chance to improve ourselves and our lot, even if we start our afterlife in one of the lowest and darkest of places. We make our own assessments of our lives and deeds.

THE ASTRAL PLANE

According to the dead (and to the Timestream ethereals), the afterlife exists on the astral plane, which has no natural landscape of its own. It is a state of being that is white and formless, composed of astral matter that molds itself to thought. This may be the reason why some people who have visits to the afterlife and come back, such as in a near-death experience, report seeing things that conform to their expectations. The dead tell us they can manifest whatever they think in terms of their appearance, movements, and environment and whom they wish to see. The astral matter responds instantly. They also say that, when they are ready, they have the ability to move on to higher realms that are beyond the ability of the living to understand.

So, the "rules" of the afterlife are different than on Earth: Things can manifest instantly, and there is no passage of time. Things simply "are."

The astral plane has different levels:

1. The lower astral, a dense place for bad souls that is unpleasant and also inhabited by entities who

like to masquerade and toy with the living. The spirit communications from this level are misleading, we are told.

2. An idealized Earth-like setting created by thought, a resting place for many, especially those who are confused by their transition. Here the newly dead make their life assessments and try to ascend to the third level. Some need help doing so, from either the living or dead or both. Spirit communications from here are unreliable.

3. Summerland, a paradise-like state, also created by thought and very similar to Earth, but idealized. Souls can spend a long time here, then either decide to reincarnate or seek to move up to the fourth level. Spirit communications from here are high quality.

4. Mental and causal planes, lacking much of the material trappings of the thought-created lower planes, a place where ideas and inspirations are born and talents are perfected. Ideas from the mental and causal planes can be transmitted to the living via dreams, inspiration, visionary experience, and so on.

5. A completely nonphysical state difficult to reach except by great teachers and religious figures and ascended masters.

6. Cosmic consciousness, a unity of souls, embodying human concepts of deity.

7. Integration into the All That Is, complete submergence of individuality into the whole.

Immediately after death, most souls first go to one of the first three levels, then eventually move on to the upper levels. The upper three levels are hard for the living to fully comprehend, and communication from there with the living becomes rarer and more difficult. Also, souls who reach the higher levels often lose their interest in talking to the living. Perhaps this explains why contact is lost with some souls.

THE AFTERLIFE LIFE

Assuming we make to it to the mid-astral level, then what happens to us? According to the dead, we find a place similar to the Earth left behind but with different physics. After a period of rest, we jump into our new life. We can live in a house, work at a job, have relationships and a family, and share common interests with others. So far it doesn't sound much different from life on Earth. But there are significant changes.

The afterlife body isn't flesh and blood but astral, composed of spiritual matter, and so we have the ability to take on our favorite appearance. Most people opt for a youthful look in their prime of life. We have the ability to move at will through time and space and think things into being. We mix with other souls according to the interests we had on Earth. We may, at least for a time, volunteer to help other newly arrived souls adjust to the afterlife. We might also participate in communication efforts with the living.

We may be unsettled to find that all of our thoughts and emotions are transparent—it is impossible to hide them in the afterlife, so no fibbing or even "white lying." We have to learn to be honest at all times and take on the challenge of purifying the inner self to eliminate deceit and duplicity.

At some point, we can elect to reincarnate, especially if we can't get rid of negative thoughts. Reincarnation is not limited to Earth. There are many worlds, dimensions, and life-forms to experience.

At some point, we may have contact with the ethereals, souls from the higher, subtle realms. They have refined themselves to exist in states of love, peace, and beauty, immersed in light. They take on ethereal bodies of light, looking like what the living might describe as angels. In order to reach these levels, we must purge ourselves of negativity.

The highest realms are literally beyond the comprehension of the human mind. The living cannot perceive the occupants of these levels, except when the entities reduce their vibration and move down to a lower level. The points where dimensions and astral planes intersect are called "dispassing" places or points.

Hans Bender, an eminent German psychologist and parapsychologist who became an avid researcher of Electronic Voice Phenomena, died in 1991 and in 1994 left text messages on the computer screen of his fellow researcher Adolf Homes. One of Bender's messages read:

> Your system of reality is one of countless others. All are happening at the same time. The "frequency" of our own reality is so short that it can not be perceived by you. It is far outside the range of electromagnetic wavelengths and has nothing to do with it anymore. The real system of all being consists of the continuous changes of all consciousness. This fact is the foundation of the differences in logic and makes communication to you and with other life forms more difficult.
>
> Please, do not visualize that we exist above you such as in "heaven." The concepts "above" and "below" are products of your mind. The soul does not swing upwards, it exists in the center and orients itself in every direction . . .
>
> Things you create with your mind are always part of your post mortal life whether they seem real or not. This is also true of your religion. You shall always find what you created in your mind, for instance, a benevolent god or an evil devil. Between them are countless facets. Therefore concentrate on the depth of your consciousness and on what you consider positive and good.
>
> Good and evil do not exist for me anymore. The fear of evil is merely a mass projection here and on

earth. The core of my personality consists of many selves . . . Because of this I have a much greater psychological experience and the forms of my awareness are richer than yours.

According to the dead, once we get adjusted to the afterlife we discover that there is no single afterlife but simultaneous and timeless realities; parallel worlds where doubles of ourselves live; probabilities; and a tremendous creative force of thought. If each of us realized even to a small degree how powerful our thoughts are, we would do immediate internal housekeeping.

Many deceased communicators have criticized organized religion, citing cruel gods, fear, ignorance, and limitation as problems associated with it. They emphasize how hard it is for them to contact us, that the process on their end relies more on thought, and that windows for communication are narrow and the energy involved runs down after a time, like a depleted battery.

The dead also tell us that certain things in the afterlife are far beyond our comprehension and are too difficult to explain. To skeptics, that's a dodge. If the dead are truly interested in helping the living become more enlightened, why don't they just come clean with direct answers to our questions?

However, the answers we seek may be far more complicated than we realize. We tend to see things in black and white. Our concepts of reality and even our very thinking processes may not be able to grasp certain complexities beyond the veil. It may be true that we will not discover some things until we arrive in the afterlife and even then we may only know a little more than we do now—at least until we advance to higher levels. At that point we may go beyond communicating with the living.

These concepts of the afterlife are exciting and refreshing. It makes far more sense that the afterlife is a place of dynamic change and limitless potential rather than an eternal sentence of good or bad. This afterlife places more responsibility on the shoulders of the individual. The afterlife is not dependent on just what a person does during life but keeps changing in accordance to ongoing choices made by the soul. Some may find that difficult and even threatening, preferring to leave everything in the hands of a divine judge who conducts a trial and pronounces an eternal verdict. If the astral plane is fluid, that type of afterlife exists, too— but only until a soul realizes that such beliefs are a prison and the horizons are much broader. Friedrich Jürgenson changed his own personal views on the afterlife as a result of his research. "The concepts of Heaven, Hell and Devil as found in the Holy Scriptures have proved to be nonexistent," Bender said bluntly. "Humanity alone in its imperfect imagination has created the likeness of a personal God. . . . Therefore do not expect from the dead tracts on political morality, philosophy or ethics. All this mental shadow boxing has lost its significance on the other side . . . we have to leave it behind on our deathbed whether we want to or not, along with our checkbook."

ANIMALS IN THE AFTERLIFE

Whenever we talk about pets in the afterlife on *Coast to Coast*, the phone lines really light up. Pets have a special heart bond with us, and when one passes, the grief can be just as deep and profound as that felt over the loss of a human loved one, and for some people even more so. Pets love us so completely, so unconditionally, that when we lose them the sadness is nearly unbearable.

We have a lot of callers who report that their departed pets come back to visit them. Sometimes they are only heard or sensed, but sometimes they are seen, either as ghosts or in lifelike form. Joshua P. Warren, who has a regular segment on my show, was visited by the ghost of his miniature dachshund, Nellie, soon after her passing. Her whimpers and barks were heard in empty rooms in his house. He also could hear the sound of her little toenails on the hardwood floor. Nellie was not visible, but her presence was quite strong.

A caller named Liz told me on air one night about the return of her beloved dog, Woofty. Liz would awaken every night at 3:00 A.M. and see Woofty sitting by Liz's favorite chair, wagging his tail, sometimes with his leash in his mouth.

These sorts of experiences are reported so often that it is hard to dismiss them as wishful thinking. If dead people can visit us, surely our pets can as well. Besides personal testimonies, we do have ample evidence that animals survive death, from mediumistic communications, apparitions, animal communicators—and Electronic Voice Phenomena. Pets are also in their prime and peak in the afterlife. Many people expect to be reunited with their beloved pets, who are just as much members of the family as human beings.

Since the early days of spirit communications research, people have recorded the phantom sounds of animals: dogs barking, cats meowing, birds singing, and so forth. Comments California EVP researcher Margaret Downey, "It is important for some people to know their animals are okay, just as it is to know about people."

It's comforting to hear your beloved dog barking from the Beyond. But what if you could communicate with your deceased pets—and they talked back to you *in your own language?* Sound fantastic? The rules are different in the afterlife. Spirit communicators say that the consciousness of everything in the afterlife expands: the ability of humans to communicate with animals and plants, and the consciousness of animals as well.

In the 1980s, German researcher Klaus Schreiber reported that he captured an EVP audio recording of a voice identifying itself as that of Jakob, his deceased pet crow. Since 1998 Anabela Cardoso, researcher and editor of the *ITC Journal,* has received several direct radio voice communications from Nisha, one of her Doberman pinschers who resides on the Other Side.

Cardoso has reported other deceased animals who communicate in voice. For example, Brazilian researcher

Sonia Rinaldi recorded a parrot, Lorinho, the former pet of her colleague Claudio Brasil. The parrot delivered a message in Portuguese.

Perhaps we should not be so surprised that animals can take on language in the afterlife. People who are tuned into their pets, and psychics who work as animal communicators, know quite well that animals do communicate telepathically. Tuned-in humans know how their pets are feeling and what they are thinking, via the exchange of images, emotional nuances, and intuitive impressions. Even words pop into the human mind to convey what is on an animal's mind. In turn, humans can convey their thoughts, emotions, and intentions. All a person has to do is think, *Walk*, or visualize a walk and a dog will react, regardless of whether or not the timing falls into routine. And how many pets know when a ride in the car is not for errands or fun—but for a trip to the veterinarian? They must sense a person's intention.

In fact, the telepathic bond between people and animals has been studied scientifically by biologist Rupert Sheldrake. Sheldrake focused on pets who anticipate when their owners are coming home and found significant results demonstrating a knowing ten to thirty minutes in advance. Variables such as random times, vehicles, and routes did not matter. Sheldrake concluded that people and their pets have an empathic bond that enables two-way telepathic communication. The results of his study were published in his book *Dogs That Know When Their Owners Are Coming Home* (1999).

Sheldrake also studied other interesting interspecies communications cases, such as a parrot who commented on the thoughts and dreams of his owner. Aimee Morgana had given the parrot, N'kisi, extensive speech training using techniques called "sentence frames" and "cognitive mapping." N'kisi developed a vocabulary of hundreds of words and learned how to speak in complete grammatical sentences; he uttered thousands of original sentences. Morgana recorded numerous telepathic communications with the bird. In tests conducted by Sheldrake, the parrot responded to Morgana's thoughts while she looked at pictures in a distant location.

Neither Sheldrake nor Morgana were involved with afterlife animal spirit communications. However, we can speculate that where consciousness expands in boundless directions, those interspecies telepathic impressions can be transformed into spoken language, which in turn can be transmitted to the living via Electronic Voice Phenomena. Human beings and animals develop tremendous bonds of love that are just as strong as human-to-human love—and for some, even stronger. The force of love may be a key factor in the connection. Animal communicators say that love and empathy enable a soul-to-soul communication and rapport, on both sides of the veil.

The animal-human Electronic Voice Phenomena may be predecessors to better interspecies communication on this side of the veil. Our advances in subtle technologies, including those aimed at bridging dimensions, may make interspecies communication a reality in the near future.

One of the most unusual animal communications from the afterlife was received by a French couple, Maryvonne and Yvon Dray, who recorded their daughter's dog, Tuly, announcing, *"Moi, j'comprends tout"* ("Me, I understand everything"). That's more than many humans acknowledge once they make it to the Other Side!

SEX IN THE AFTERLIFE

A glimpse into the afterlife would not be complete without considering a question that almost everyone wants to ask but doesn't: do we have sex after we're dead?

"Yes, there is sex in the afterlife, people carry on the same as they do here . . ."

"There is sex after death, but people do it differently, they don't have bodies anymore . . ."

"There is *no* sex in the afterlife, people leave that behind when they go into spirit . . ."

"There is an exchange of energy; it's better than sex . . ."

"People can come back after they die and have sex with the living . . ."

I hear all of the preceding comments—and more—whenever the topic comes up concerning what life is like in the afterlife. Some of these are offered as opinions; some are stated emphatically as facts. One thing is clear: there is *no* agreement on whether or not human beings can pursue one of their favorite activities once they have died. Religion, which has always been uncomfortable on the subject of sex, has little to offer us as a guide. The dead, however, are not shy on the subject. After all, sex is one of the most fundamental, powerful, and pleasurable ways that human beings communicate with each other. In the afterlife, does this communication remain physical—or does it take on new forms no longer requiring biological interaction?

Ancient and Religious Views

We don't have the space here to delve into all the religious, philosophical, and metaphysical entanglements about afterlife sex, but a little background is helpful.

According to the Greeks, sex after death was out—as were all physical pleasures. The Greeks envisioned a gloomy afterlife in which the shades of the dead longed for physical stimulation.

Zoroastrianism, an ancient religion that originated in Persia before Christianity, held that sex is possible, but the souls of the dead would evolve away from it. They would gravitate toward better things to do.

There is little dogma about sex in the afterlife in Judaism. The Torah indicates that the righteous will be reunited with their loved ones, without going into details.

Islam allows for physical pleasures for the righteous in heaven.

Christianity has been especially uncomfortable about sex, anywhere, in life or the afterlife. Officially, there is no sex in heaven, a belief based on the teachings of Jesus, such as the words attributed to him in Matthew 22:30.

When the Sadducees tried to discredit Jesus by questioning him about marriage and the resurrection, Jesus said, "At the resurrection people will neither marry nor be given in marriage; they will be like the angels in heaven." The implication is, with eternal life, there is no need to procreate and thus no need to have sex or the institution of marriage.

Some modern interpretations of this statement hold that Jesus was referring strictly to marriage, not necessarily to sex, which is inherently spiritual. ". . . [T]here is certainly sex in Heaven simply because there are human beings in Heaven," according to philosophy professor Peter Kreeft. "As we have seen, sexuality, like race and unlike clothes, is an essential aspect of our identity, spiritual as well as physical. Even if sex were not spiritual, there would be sex in Heaven because of the resurrection of the body. The body is not a mistake to be unmade or a prison cell to be freed from, but a divine work of art designed to show forth the soul as the soul is to show forth God, in splendor and glory and overflow of generous superfluity."

Jesus compared the heavenly humans to angels. Do angels have sex? In certain texts, they do—with people. In the book of Genesis, there is a brief mention of the Watchers, who are angels assigned with the duty of watching over human beings. Some of them lusted after women. They decided to desert their posts, come down to Earth, and cohabit with the women. Their offspring were bloodthirsty cannibals called Nephilim. Not a pretty picture. As a result, God cleansed the planet with the Flood. The book of Enoch, which was excluded from the biblical canon, goes into much more detail about this story. There are several known versions of the book, and historians estimate that they were written by a collection of anonymous authors sometime between the second century BCE and sixth century CE. Jesus may have perceived sexless angels and eventually sexless humans, but the people of Jesus' day and later conceived of transdimensional and trans-species sexual relations.

Taught that dead people will get their bodies back in heaven after the Judgment Day, early Christians inevitably asked about sex in heaven. Saint Augustine, one of the great fathers of the church—and one who struggled to reconcile sex with spiritual matters—opined that we will get our bodies back complete in heaven, but the sexual organs will be for aesthetics only, to restore the perfection of the male and female bodies. The sexual organs will not function because they will not be needed, he said. One might wonder, *Why have them at all?* But perhaps incomplete heavenly bodies would have been a difficult sell to the pagan masses who were lobbied for conversion—and whose gods were quite sensual. Augustine nonetheless still tried to put sexual arousal in a different perspective. He asserted: "There will be female parts, not suited to their old use, but to a new beauty, and this will not arouse the lust of the beholder, for there will be not lust, but it will inspire praise of the wisdom and goodness of God."

Saint Thomas Aquinas, a medieval theologian and one of the greatest philosophers of the church, wrote aplenty on sex in the world of the living. As for the afterlife, he agreed with Saint Augustine on functionless sexual organs. Aquinas said that those who go to heaven will be in spiritual union with God. No one, evidently, will need or even think about sex in such an exalted state.

But is such a heaven exalted—or boring? Mark Twain, quite the outspoken humorist, found the prospect of a sex-free heaven quite dull. "Of all the delights of this world man cares most for sexual intercourse," Twain said in his *Notebook* (1906). "He will go to any length for it—risk fortune, character, reputation, life itself. And what do you think he [God] has done? He has left it out of his heaven! Prayer takes its place."

England's Queen Victoria was a contemporary of Twain's. We associate the period of her reign, 1837–1901, the so-called "Victorian era," with straitlaced morals and pinched views on sexuality—but Victoria herself evidently looked forward to sex in the afterlife. In 1840, at age twenty-one, she married her first cousin Albert, the son of Ernest I, Duke of Saxe-Coburg and Gotha. They had nine children. Albert died in 1861, and Victoria went into perpetual mourning, wearing black for the rest of her life. She was buried in her treasured bridal veil in anticipation of a reunion with her beloved.

Mormonism, founded by Joseph Smith Jr. in the nineteenth century, comes down squarely on the side of sex in heaven—but only for the chosen ones. A special marriage ceremony on earth seals an everlasting union in heaven, where love, sex, and procreation continue. The spiritual children of such unions are sent into physical bodies for their trials of mortality.

We've just touched the very tip of the iceberg here, and you can see the complications humans have experienced over the course of history in trying to grapple with the subject of sex. It seems that no matter what religion has had to say about sex, many people still wonder about whether or not it is possible in the afterlife. If we continue on and if we are reunited with our loved ones, wouldn't it be logical to have some form of sexual pleasure? Even outside of mainstream religion, people have had difficulty confronting the subject.

The eighteenth-century mystic Emanuel Swedenborg, who made numerous out-of-body trips to the afterlife while in deep trance states, said that in heaven humans become angels. He saw a three-tiered, progressive afterlife. In the first stage, the dead carry on much as they do on earth, but without the problems. They marry, work at jobs, live in communities, and so on. In the second stage, they continue doing the same, but in a more idealized state. In the third stage, they evolve into a more spiritual and celestial sphere. However, Swedenborg said that heavenly marriage is more a union of mind, not of any kind of body, and the procreation involved is not children but "good and truth." A man and woman do not have a wedding in the earthly sense but are consorts who join minds together to form a single angel. Adultery is considered heinous and belonging to hell—a state, by the way, that human beings choose through their actions in life. There is no divine judgment and sentencing in the Swedenborgian view.

The Dead Speak Out on Sex

Such idealized unions are reinforced in many, but not all, mediumistic communications, in which the dead say that they have love for others, including the intimate partners they had in life, but it is expressed more as a blending of energy and soul on a higher spiritual level. The actual biological urge is either unimportant or nonexistent. This blending of energies is described in the out-of-body-experience literature by astral travelers. Astral sex can be experienced by the living and is characterized by an ecstasy far greater than physical sex.

George W. Meek, who created the controversial Spiricom, believed that marriage exists in the afterlife, but it is not a "compelling need" because there is no procreation of children. Without the need for offspring, "there is no functional need for human intercourse" and thus no afterlife sex, he stated adamantly in *After We Die, What Then?* (1980). However, spirits informed him that there is a lot of "funny business" going on in the lower astral realm—not only sex but orgies. Sleeping living people sometimes attend these sex fests, which drain their energy, he said.

Meek's view is contradicted by the luminary dead belonging to Timestream. They said that after death human souls go to the astral plane, where they encounter a realm much like the Earth but more paradise-like, with different laws of physics. We asked Mark Macy, who had worked closely with Timestream, if the luminary dead had provided any details about physical intimacy. "The Timestream spirit group told us that they have bodies just like the bodies they'd had on Earth, but at the prime of life," Macy said. "Their bodies have all the organs their physical bodies had, including sex organs. Yes, two willing partners can enjoy sex, but no one gets pregnant."

The Timestream group also said that the dead continue on much as they lived on earth, with spouses, families, jobs, and other activities. However, the dead are not bound by time and space and they can shed their astral bodies and merge with the environment. They may spend a long time on the astral level, but at some point they are motivated to either reincarnate or ascend to a higher spiritual plane. Ascension means becoming increasingly ethereal to the point of pure consciousness. Obviously, sex at that point is not even a footnote of interest.

Medium James Van Praagh also perceives a heaven that is "the other side of our physical world," though much more vivid and colorful. "Heaven is a place where we can stroll in a garden, or ride a bicycle, or row a boat," he said in *Talking to Heaven* (1997). "As a matter of fact, we can do anything in heaven that we want as long as we have earned it."

As I mentioned, sex in the afterlife is vast territory, and we could devote an entire book to it. Spirit communications seldom mention sex unless the living ask specifically about it, and even then the answers can be short and cryptic. Instead, the dead—at least those who talk to researchers—place more of an emphasis on ideas, ideals, philosophy, and advancements of spirit and of soul. Actually, that is not surprising. An analogy is the workplace. The intent of research in spirit communication is to prove the afterlife and find ways to develop better communication links and methods. Whether or not the dead are able to have sex isn't usually on the discussion table.

Human experience, however, indicates that interest in physical sex continues on after death—except the dead go looking for it back in the world of the living. Sexual encounters with the dead may seem laughable on the surface, but paranormal investigators frequently encounter testimonies about it, usually from people who sleep in haunted hotels and inns or move into homes that have unusual paranormal activity. Experiences also happen in people's own homes, especially after the death of a spouse. The people who have such experiences are often too embarrassed to talk about them in public. But "ghost sex" does happen, and, Rosemary estimates from her own research, it happens far more frequently than most people might imagine.

Experiences range from intimate touching to complete sex. The "ghost" feels like real flesh and blood, quite solid. Sometimes the experiencers feel "something" slide into bed after they have retired or they awaken from sleep to find themselves with an invisible partner. There are possible explanations for some of these encounters, such as repressed sexual tension, vivid dreaming, and, in the case of bereavement, grief and longing that get projected out. However, not all ghost sex experiences can be readily explained. We also have precedents well established in folklore and supernatural lore, beliefs around the world that the dead can come back to have sex with the living.

Experiencers confess a range of reactions. Some are shocked and terrified. Others admit they enjoy the experience. This is especially the case where the visitor is a departed and greatly missed lover or spouse. Sometimes the encounters are amusing. A woman once told Rosemary about an unexpected amorous ghost who came to her while she slept in a haunted hotel. She was alone, lying on her side, and awakened to the sensation of a physical body next to her and behind her in bed. She was shocked to feel physical touch. After she got over the shock, the touching was quite pleasant, and so she let herself enjoy the experience. "I would have gone all the way," she said, "except I couldn't find a zipper!"

There is little agreement on exactly what a visiting "ghost" is, especially one capable of manifesting the sensations of physical contact. Is a ghost a remnant or a shell of someone who has died? An earthbound soul? An astral body vehicle for a disembodied spirit on the Other Side to visit the earth plane? Perhaps they include all of those.

One of the strangest accounts of sex between the living and the dead has the makings of a supernatural soap opera: it involves reincarnation and an illicit love affair that reputedly took place more than three thousand years ago in the royal courts of ancient Egypt. The central figures were an

Englishwoman, Dorothy Eady, and Sety I, the pharaoh of Egypt in the Nineteenth Dynasty, who lived from 1306 to 1290 BCE. Jonathan Cott documented the story in *The Search for Omm Sety* (1987). Eady, born in 1904, was three years old when she suffered a head trauma and nearly died after falling down stairs. Head trauma is sometimes associated with an onset of psychic ability or visionary experiences. Little Dorothy soon began having strange dreams of an ancient land she did not recognize.

One night when she was fourteen, Eady had the shocking dream of a bizarre face bending low over her as she slept. She discovered it was the mummy of Sety I. A recurring dream happened in which she was a young Egyptian girl who was being beaten with a stick for refusing to answer questions.

Eady gradually pieced together her own story and came to the conclusion that in a past life she had been a temple priestess at Abydos sworn to keep her virginity but had fallen in love with the pharaoh, a mature man in his fifties. They engaged in a torrid affair and she became pregnant. Shamed, she committed suicide.

Eady felt Sety was somehow calling to her from the afterlife, and she became obsessed with reuniting with him. She devoured everything she could find about Egypt and Sety I. At age twenty-nine, she married an Egyptian man and moved to Cairo.

Once Eady was in Egypt, her passionate and now transdimensional love affair with Sety resumed. One night she left her physical body and traveled in her astral body to the afterlife, where she met Sety. He said he would come to her and take on physical form and they could once again enjoy lovemaking. She agreed, and he visited her at night often. He told her they could marry in Amenti, the Egyptian afterlife, after she died.

Just as in an earthly soap opera, the ecstatic physical passion was not meant to last—at least for the short remaining term of Eady's life. She left her husband and went to Abydos to live at the scene of her and Sety's past lives. He told her that if they now refrained from physical sex their crime of passion would be forgiven and they could truly unite in the afterlife. He continued to visit her in material form at night, but the sex came to an end.

Eady lived out the remainder of her life in primitive conditions, keeping mostly to herself, recording her experiences with Sety in a diary. She died in 1981. We hope she found what she wanted in the everlasting afterlife.

11

Relief from Grief

One night during the broadcast of *Coast to Coast*, my producer, Tom Danheiser, and I had what may have been a visit from the dead.

First, I need to explain the setup of our studios at Premiere Radio Network in Sherman Oaks. I do the show standing up in a studio, and from where I stand I can look straight through a big glass window into Tom's production booth. That's where he takes the calls, e-mails, and Fast Blast messages from listeners and cues up callers who want to ask questions or tell their stories. Tom's booth is small, barely big enough to hold two or three people seated. Nobody on the staff besides himself needs to go in or out.

Some of the breaks are long, and we have time to go to our offices, or go to the kitchen. During the broadcast, Tom and I don't communicate except by sign language, but when we're on a break we can speak to each other over the intercom.

On this particular night, I was going through my paperwork in the studio during one of the breaks. I looked up and saw Tom—or who I thought was Tom—in the production booth. I later asked him a question over the intercom.

"I don't know," Tom said in a matter-of-fact voice. "I wasn't here."

"What do you mean, you weren't here? I just saw you in the booth," I said.

"No I wasn't—I went down to the kitchen," he said. He held up a glass of water.

I was taken aback and puzzled. I had clearly seen *someone* in the booth and he looked just like Tom. "I swear I just saw you," I said. Then something dawned on me. "Maybe it was your brother." We both agreed; it was the only explanation that fit. I hadn't imagined it, and yet Tom himself had been away for a few minutes.

Tom's younger brother passed away some years ago. We think he may have dropped in for a brief visit. The odd thing is, I saw him and Tom did not. Why is that? Wouldn't it have made more sense for Tom to be aware of him? As far as Tom knows, he has never had conscious contact with his brother, though he would like the experience and to know for certain that his brother is all right.

As strange as it may seem, that is often the way visits

from the dead happen. They occur without warning and are often quite fleeting. Sometimes the most obvious person does not get the visit. Sometimes we only see them; sometimes we can communicate with them and even touch them.

We can only speculate that some unique mix of circumstances must be in place for a visit to happen. Researchers who have studied visits from the dead describe them as having characteristics of electricity—that is, in any given situation they follow the path of least resistance in order for a visit to happen. Otherwise, visits from the dead would be more commonplace, would happen in logical fashion, and would even be created on demand. Don't most of us who have lost loved ones wish for another encounter or for certain knowledge of their well-being in the afterlife? The living are on the passive end of visits from the dead. Willing and wishing them to happen does not seem to work. But if we can perfect spirit communications technology, that could radically change. The unpredictable ghost boxes might give way to telephone-like devices and interactive video. How about an interdimensional Internet?

When the Internet became available, an information explosion occurred. Information that in the past was hard to find is now easily accessible. In addition, the Internet helps us find and connect to people, services, organizations, and businesses. Imagine what our world would be like if we had the resources of other dimensions available! The living often assume that the dead possess great knowledge just because they have gone into the afterlife. That may or may not be the case—but reliable spirit communications would prove it one way or the other. We could be in regular contact and consultation with departed scientists, philosophers, inventors, technicians, and others who could give us new information that would send our science and technology ahead by light-years. We could learn from other life-forms as well.

WORKING WITH THE BEREAVED

One of the major reasons why many people start experimenting in spirit communications is to contact a dead loved one. Grief is a powerful motivator. Tom and Lisa Butler, the directors of the ATransC, report that many of their members find the organization in the process of searching for ways to contact the dead.

People often turn first to a medium. If they do not seek out a personal consultation, they might attend a gallery reading, in which a medium gets impressions meant for various people in the audience. John Edward's television show *Crossing Over* was an example of the gallery reading. I attended a gallery reading done in Los Angeles by James Van Praagh and Tony Stockwell, a popular medium from the United Kingdom. In gallery readings, the messages are usually short, but they still have a powerful emotional impact upon the recipients.

An increasing number of people opt to go further with direct contact with the dead, in hopes of hearing the voices of those they have lost.

Margaret Downey is a Los Angeles–based spirit communications researcher who works with the bereaved to help them have communication with their loved ones on the Other Side. Interested in the paranormal for her entire life, Downey started experimenting with traditional Electronic Voice Phenomena in June 2005. She was successful, but often the voices were faint and hard to understand. She looked for ways to make them clearer, using background sounds such as fans, running water, crinkling aluminum foil, foreign crowd babble—anything she could think of. She tried radio sweep, EVPMaker and the Paranormal Puck, allophones and phonemes.

Downey found she got the best results with radio sweep and with EVPMaker allophones—and that different entities come through different equipment and techniques. With EVPMaker, Downey has communicated with an entity named Arthur, who describes himself as "ex-human" and says he can communicate with multiple people at the same time. Arthur never claimed to have incarnated on Earth, and his messages are full of information about portals, spirit elders, and metaphysical topics. Apparently there are things Arthur either does not wish to discuss or is forbidden from discussing, for sometimes his response is to cite "Article Eight," the nature of which remains a mystery. He does exhibit a sense of humor. Once he told Downey, "You humans are so beautiful—and dumb."

"Oh, so I'm beautiful?" Downey responded.

"And dumb," he replied glibly.

For all of his knowledge and amusements, however,

Arthur has nothing to do with the human dead. "He seems to be part of an etheric group that works on communication with people, but not with contact with our dead loved ones," said Downey. "They are off in a separate space."

Downey's dominant contact with the dead comes through radio sweep. She favors manual radio sweep, which produces a background noise similar to traditional EVP. She also uses the same model of MiniBox favored by Rosemary.

"I have two technicians on the Other Side, David and Patrick, who work with me constantly and faithfully," Downey said. "I have not determined where they originate from, but they are part of a tech group. When I am doing Electronic Voice Phenomena, they talk constantly in the background with advice on changing the channel, switching the uplink, commenting on whether or not the network is working, and providing me with instructions on changing my settings. At the same time, they are helping the loved ones come through."

David and Patrick say they know who Arthur is—they call him "Arthur the tech"—and he is "decent people" and they support Downey's working with him. But Arthur says he does not know who David and Patrick are. Perhaps they are in different dimensions that have only select intersections, or "dispassing" points, as the Timestream communicators called them.

Downey decided to focus on communicating with the dead to help the bereaved and became a certified practitioner with the ATransC. In 2008 she met Lisa Winther-

Huston of Los Angeles, who was producing a documentary about afterlife communication. Winther-Huston has extensive experience in film and television production and twenty years' experience as an intuitive channel. They were inspired to work together, which was reinforced by EVP messages in their first session.

Downey and Winther-Huston work as a team to conduct sessions for people who wish to contact their loved ones. A typical session runs four to five hours and involves video and audio recording. The recording is done in increments of about two minutes, with immediate review, so that the clients can react and respond. "It is not the same as being on the telephone," said Downey. "It is simulated real time, a conversation in delay, because we stop and do the reviews of the recordings as we go. We'll do it until the person feels emotionally complete with the session."

Downey asks for names of the dead and the living present and questions about the dead person's well-being, who they are with in the afterlife, and what their world is like. Usually there is at least one meaningful response in a session, and often there are many.

Reactions of the living cover a range: shock, disbelief, excitement, tears, relief, and sometimes skepticism. Overall, said Downey, "there is quite a bit of healing. Most people just want to know if their loved one is all right, and do they know we are trying to talk to them. Some people have burning unanswered questions, and they feel more balanced when they get an answer."

One of Downey and Winther-Huston's clients was

Bob, a writer and director who sought communication with his deceased parents. Prior to the session, he admitted to being nervous about what to expect. Neither Lisa nor Margaret knew anything about Bob's family, including the names of his parents and other relatives. Responses were immediate and Bob could clearly hear the names of family members being spoken. He went away from the session certain he had engaged in real communication.

Sometimes poltergeist effects erupt in the environment during a session. Objects have been knocked over, sometimes in weirdly orchestrated ways. During the session with Bob, an unknown real-time male voice said, "Answer the phone, Bob." Immediately his telephone rang and he got up to answer it. Another voice said, "Push it over," just as Bob walked past a framed photo of his parents sitting on a table. The photo fell over. "They orchestrated that," said Downey. "They were trying hard to come through and show us we go on past our physical being."

Since 2001 Brazilian researcher Sonia Rinaldi, coordinator of Associação Nacional de Transcomunicadores (ANT), has been making real-time phone calls to the dead, primarily to children in order to help their grieving parents and other relatives. Mediumistic from a young age, Rinaldi was naturally attracted to spirit communications. In 1994 she received a "phone call from the dead" from Konstantin Raudive and Carlos de Almeida, a deceased Brazilian researcher. Rinaldi and other researchers were told that the spirit world has a variety of apparatuses for making calls to earthly telephones, including devices that had microphones and sound systems and some that were like telephones themselves.

Rinaldi has her own technique of a telephone connected to a computer to record real-time phone calls between the living and the dead. The technology is controlled by the Beyond, but the call is not from the Beyond, according to Rinaldi. The dead communicators enter the terrestrial phone.

The spirit communicators modulate a noise matrix created by live people who are enunciating the sounds of language read from a list. For attempts to contact specific deceased persons, Rinaldi uses gender- and age-appropriate readers. For communication with a dead child, a living child reads the phonetic sounds. Results are immediate, and sometimes the communicators start speaking before the experimenters, as though they know what is coming.

Rinaldi works with parents to record EVP sessions directly with their deceased child over her system. A typical conversation lasts twelve to fifteen minutes. Questions that have been prepared in advance are asked, and ten to fifteen seconds are left for answers. Rinaldi provides the parents with recordings so that they can assess the voice and the information.

According to Rinaldi, those working on the Other Side to make the communication bridge possible are part of "stations" that serve only particular areas on earth. Her system works only with Brazilians. Researchers in other countries, notably Spain, Uruguay, and Argentina, have followed her model to create their own communications stations.

Some of the dead children contacted by Rinaldi say they go on living in their parents' house. They also seem to occupy a parallel space around Rinaldi's house, along with other spirits who are part of the transmission station.

THE BIG CIRCLE

The death of her daughter sent Martha Pierce Copeland of Atlanta into Electronic Voice Phenomena and eventually on to found one of the leading spirit communications support groups for the grieving, especially parents who have lost children. Copeland lost twenty-year-old Cathy to an automobile accident on December 23, 2001. As an eerie foreshadowing, Cathy and her cousin Rachel were in a serious auto accident three weeks prior to that. The close call prompted them to make a pact that whoever would die first would make an effort to communicate from the Other Side. Three weeks later, Cathy was killed in another accident. Martha was devastated.

The first contact with Cathy occurred five months later, when Rachel, missing her cousin, tried to communicate with Cathy via Electronic Voice Phenomena recorded on her computer. After many tries over many hours, a message came through. Rachel called Copeland and said, "Aunt Martha, I've got Cathy on my computer!" Then Rachel's mother, Martha's sister, called and said, "You've got to come over and listen to this—it's Cathy's voice."

The message was a faint and scratchy, "I'm still here," followed by an unknown male voice saying, "How do you know they can hear?" But Cathy's voice was immediately recognizable. Copeland was both stunned and excited. It was unbelievable to her that she could hear her daughter speaking from the afterlife: "I'm still here."

Copeland tried Electronic Voice Phenomena herself with her own computer. Results were not immediate, but eventually Copeland got her own message: "Mama, I'm right here." Later that night, Martha awakened hearing Cathy's voice in her mind: *Mom, you've got to try again . . . You do not need to use the computer. You can hear me in your head.*

Via the Internet, Copeland found others like her doing Electronic Voice Phenomena. Grieving mothers came to her house to try Electronic Voice Phenomena. Eventually, they all heard the voices of their children. Copeland joined the American Association of Electronic Voice Phenomena, now the ATransC, and became active in the EVP community.

In communications via computer and digital and tape recorders, Cathy said she and her spirit friends—other children trying to communicate with their families—call themselves the Big Circle. Copeland organized the Recording Circle Bridge to the Afterlife to connect to the Big Circle. Participants can join in anywhere at set times for a group meditation, recording, and sharing experience.

Copeland favors one recorder for her work that is her special connection to Cathy. Martha does not allow anyone else to handle it and takes it with her wherever she goes. Once she went on a trip and forgot to take it along.

When she returned home, there was a message from Cathy on it: "Where's Mom?"

For the grieving, the overriding desire is for contact. Their evidence rests more with personal articles of faith rather than data a scientist would appreciate. There are researchers who navigate the territory in between, striving to keep up with solid technological advancements that in turn deliver messages to the bereaved.

A major figure in the Big Circle was Debbie Caruso of Staten Island, New York. Born in Brooklyn, Caruso was a jeweler who owned her own business—and who had little interest in the paranormal until death touched her life.

In 2004 she and her family were on vacation in Mexico and became involved in an automobile accident that killed Caruso's sixteen-year-old son, Joey, and critically injured her daughter, Alexa. Alexa was hospitalized and in a coma. When she awakened, Debbie had the painful task of informing Alexa of her brother's death. "He can't be dead," she protested. "He speaks to me every day." That was the first sign that Joey could reach out from the Other Side.

Caruso looked for other signs such as feathers and physical clues that Joey's presence was still with her. Then someone told her about Electronic Voice Phenomena and suggested that she might be able to communicate with Joey. Her first reaction was, "This can't be true." She went home, turned on her computer, and spoke into the recorder. A man answered, giving his name and saying he was one hundred years old. Shocked, Caruso stopped, but curiosity compelled her to try again. As she experimented more, she connected with Joey. In the first recording of his voice, a woman's voice seemed to prompt him, "Speak to her." Then Joey said, "Ma?"

Caruso recorded numerous messages from Joey and also of other children of members of the Big Circle. One of her most meaningful messages came on September 11, 2007, the twentieth birthday of Joey, when he left an Electronic Voice Phenomenon saying, "Ma, I love you."

Caruso passed herself on January 22, 2010, at age fifty, of cancer. "She is an amazingly beautiful soul and she was a talented and dedicated researcher," said Margaret Downey. "She wanted more than anything for two things: to see her son Joey again and to know exactly what it is like on the Other Side. Now she is getting to experience her dream."

Within days of her passing, Caruso was communicating with Downey and other researchers. Downey captured an image of Caruso's face in her spirit photography and also captured radio sweep Electronic Voice Phenomena that went like this:

> DOWNEY: Debbie, are you there?
> UNKNOWN MAN: She's in the Big Circle.
> DOWNEY: I heard them say you're in the Big Circle.
> CARUSO: It's me and Joseph!
> UNKNOWN MAN: Debbie is not dead.

The main message that we get over and over again from the Other Side is, the dead are not dead but live on in another form. No matter how many times we ask the question about survival, that is the answer we get. When are we going to listen?

Let's go to Italy now and look in on another researcher who has worked with the grieving and who has undergone some astounding tests for authenticity.

12

Spirit Forensics

In a room dimly lit by a 25-watt blue lightbulb, a small group of people sit in hushed anticipation of one of the paranormal wonders of the modern world: direct real-time conversations with the dead over the radio. Present are parents grieving over the untimely loss of their children, an international collection of paranormal researchers, mediums, technical and scientific experts, and the curious. The location is Grosseto, Italy, and the master of ceremonies is the legendary Marcello Bacci, who has successfully pierced the veil to the Beyond for more than forty years. His setup is no Frankensteinian laboratory full of Tesla coils, Koenig ultrasound generators, or shrieking ghost boxes. Rather, his star piece of equipment is a humble 1950s Normende vacuum-tube (valve) radio in a wooden cabinet.

On this night, the anticipation is higher than usual, for Bacci's work is going to be put to the test. It is not the first time experts have tried to debunk or unmask the secrets behind the voices he gets. In the past, the experts have gone away awed, puzzled, and confounded. Will it be the same again tonight, with an unusual test at hand? Will physics once again be "turned upside down"?

Bacci, a quiet man in his seventies who has never sought the limelight, focuses his attention. He turns on his radio and selects shortwave band, slowly turning the tuning control to a range between seven and nine megahertz. He explains in Italian that he is searching for "good white noise." The searching goes on for nearly twenty minutes, and then Bacci announces, "I feel them—they will come!"

He stops tuning and a white noise fills the room. The white noise changes to an eerie sound like rushing wind or beating waves—or the audio landscape of another dimension. Then this noise dies down, replaced by a rise of voices that pour through the radio loudspeakers. The first voices speak Italian, followed by Spanish. Bacci welcomes the spirits and tells them they can also speak in Portuguese and English.

For the next hour, five or six voices (one of them sounding female, the rest male) address the sitters in English, Italian, and Spanish. Their voices are clear but possess the weird intonations, rhythms, and sentence constructions familiar in paranormal voice communications. There are occasional sound distortions. Still, the thirty-seven sitters can understand approximately 70 percent of the communications. The spirits address them by name in a language they understand. The spirits switch languages with ease, sometimes answering in a different language from the one they are queried in and sometimes switching languages in the middle of their answers. This multilingual ease has been well demonstrated in the past among many spirit communications researchers.

It is time for the test, a follow-up to an earlier test.

In the earlier test, two vacuum tubes, or valves, were removed from the radio that controlled frequency modulations. As a result, there was a complete absence of any signal, including shortwave. The paranormal voices carried on, demonstrating that they were not originating on radio transmissions nor were they being fraudulently produced.

In the aftermath of that test, critics still contended that the remaining three valves in the radio could have produced sound in other wave bands. So, tonight, while the voices are talking, all five valves will be removed from the radio.

An hour into the session, the voices are going strong. Radio technician Franco Santi reaches in and removes the five valves, laying them out for all witnesses to see. The radio now has no way to receive any normal signals whatsoever. The voices carry on as though nothing is amiss!

Then Bacci does something unexpected and un-planned—he shuts the radio's power off. For eleven long seconds, there is silence. Then a rushing air sound and a noise like whiplashes comes over the loudspeakers. At twenty-one seconds, a spirit voice resumes speaking, as clear as before but slower in cadence. The voice speaks for twenty-three seconds, followed by whistling and rushing sounds for twelve seconds. More silence follows, and then fifty-three seconds later the rushing sound resumes simul-taneously with a weak male voice saying in Italian, "You are great!" The entire phenomenon on a nonfunctioning radio lasts two minutes and twenty seconds.

Bacci turns the radio back on, but there is only silence, and the experiment ends.

During the time the radio was off, Santi had examined its interior with a flashlight. He continues to do so, turn-ing the radio at angles for the witnesses to see as he shines the beam of the light inside.

Once again, there is no natural explanation for the voices.

IS IT THE MACHINE OR THE MEDIUM?

How does Bacci achieve such astounding success, and how has he managed to do so for so many years? When Bacci works, he touches the wooden cabinet of the radio, a physi-cal connection that seems to facilitate the bridge. He coaxes the communicators. But if others try to use the equipment when Bacci is not present, there are no results. The key may be in his natural mediumistic ability.

Paolo Presi, an aeronautical engineer and a leading member of a paranormal research facility called Il Laboratorio in Bologna, Italy, has opined that the necessity of Bacci's presence demonstrates that successful spirit communications require at least some mediumistic and psychic abilities. The valve experiment, which took place on December 5, 2004, showed that once the valves were removed, the radio became a psychically supported device. "It is my personal opinion that the phenomenon should be considered as an interactive process among a 'Mind System,'" Presi said in 2006 in a presentation at a conference sponsored by the ATransC in Atlanta.

Even as far back as the 1980s, it was obvious to Presi that attitude and openness are critical factors in the success of spirit communications. Especially, the operator must be open to the possibility of the paranormal event before it occurs. In 1983 Presi defined this mental attitude as "Inner Attentive Disposition," an openness of mind and heart. It is, he said, "an absolute prerequisite for establishing contacts with other planes of consciousness" and is "the determining factor in opening the hidden channel that connects our physical plane to the higher planes of consciousness where one day we will, I believe, again meet our loved ones." This openness may account for the high degree of success obtained by the grieving, who are so strongly motivated to achieve contact that they set aside any rational objections to the possibility.

But mediumistic ability may not be the only key. Presi suggests that the best results are obtained when a person has both mediumistic ability *and* a "deep inner conviction about the possibility of real communication with other planes of consciousness."

Parapsychologists have found attitude to be a critical factor in the experiments to prove the existence of psi. The "experimenter effect" has been well documented in parapsychology as far back as the 1930s, when researchers noticed that the expectations and biases of experimenters affected the results of their work. No matter what the controls and protocols, a mind-set can skew actual results in a positive or negative way. Similarly, the "sheep-goat effect" has been documented since 1943. Believers in psychic phenomena, the sheep, tend to score better on psi tests than goats, or nonbelievers. Spirit communicators say that consciousness on both sides of the veil plays a significant role.

THE BACCI TOUCH

Bacci has both the mediumistic ability and the deep conviction about contact. He became interested in spirit communications in 1949, when he attended his first mediumistic séance in London. The breakthroughs in Electronic Voice Phenomena intrigued him, and he began experimenting on his own with a variety of setups, eventually arriving at his valve radio tuned to a narrow shortwave band width. He produced real-time paranormal voices over a radio as early as 1970. Bacci, his colleague Luciano Capitani, and a few others worked quietly in Grosseto, rarely going public. They held "psychophonic séances" one night a week for small groups, whose ranks included many grieving parents looking for word from their children. Word of Bacci's work filtered out in the 1980s after the news broke about George Meek's Spiricom work. Researchers went to Italy to watch Bacci in action and learn about his methods.

The early voices that came over the old radio were poor in quality, at about the same acoustical level as the voices produced by Jürgenson and Raudive, but were loud enough to be heard by the participants. The voices had a unique cadence and a singing rhythm. By the end of the 1970s, the voices sounded quicker and more impulsive, probably due to a natural evolution in adaptation to the overall communication process.

A typical forty-to-sixty-minute session yielded up to one thousand words, mostly in an old Italian dialect and in a changing tempo. Sometimes the voices spoke in different languages. Sometimes the voices gave no identities but made statements such as, "The spirit is speaking to you." Even without names, the voices showed distinct differences and personalities. Usually the communicators gave parents information about their children, but sometimes the children themselves came through, using names, references, and manners of speech recognizable by their parents. Sessions often ended with a solemn and melodic choir of voices that evoked an emotional response among sitters.

Although many spirits did not identify themselves, a few showed up with regularity: Gregorio, a male named Il Saggio ("The Wise"), and a female named Cordula.

As Bacci's work progressed and improved, the séances sometimes took on more spiritistic characteristics, with rappings, materialization of balls of light, the playing of musical instruments, and other phenomena in the environment. According to Bacci, Cordula materialized; he said her hands were like a girl's with long fingernails.

PUT TO TESTS

By the early 1990s, Bacci's voices from the Beyond increased dramatically. In 1995 an experiment was conducted with engineer Carlo Trajna in which a second radio was set next to Bacci's radio, connected to the same power, with an independent aerial and tuned to the same shortwave frequency. Voices spoke on Bacci's radio, but only white noise was produced on the second one, underscoring the evident element of mediumistic ability.

Another experiment later was conducted by Mario Salvatore Festa, a physicist at Naples University, and radio technician Franco Santi, in which the two valves were removed, as mentioned earlier. The intent was to try to identify the carrier wave created by the voices. According to the spirits, the communications are made possible by "waves that are not physical." The scientists, however, hoped their measurements of electric, magnetic, and electromagnetic fields would point to the source of origination for the voices.

For Festa, the experiment was exciting but disappointing in that the origin could not be determined. The continuation of the voices after the valves were removed could not be explained. "The rule of standard physics has been turned upside down," he commented. There was no electromagnetic signature of a carrier wave for the voices when the radio was disabled. This, said Festa, validated the authenticity of the voices, for if they had come over a nearby transmitter as part of a hoax, the instruments would have registered an increase in the electric and magnetic field. Whatever the spirits were creating for a carrier wave, it was a phenomenon "completely unknown," he said. He speculated that, from a mediumistic point of view, the energy or "vibrations" from spirits were somehow transformed by the medium into electromagnetic waves, creating radio transmissions.

In 2007 Ervin László, a Hungarian professor of philosophy, reported on his attendance at one of Bacci's sessions in Italy. Bacci was still using the old Normende radio in a wooden cabinet, which he touched while coaxing the spirits to speak; many researchers feel that physical contact with their equipment facilitates the bridge. At first there came the usual sounds like heavy breathing or rushing wind, and then recognizable voices. Communicators accurately identified people present, including László; he conversed in Hungarian with unknown male and female voices. Others present recognized the identities of communicators who spoke to them. The session was punctuated by breaks filled only with the rushing-wind sound. Bacci said that the spirits were "recharging" during the breaks. After about thirty minutes, the energy of the session dissipated and Bacci brought it to a close.

SCIENTISTS EXAMINE THE VOICES

Il Laboratorio, the informal name of the Interdisciplinary Laboratory for Biopsychocybernetics Research, was established by six Italian scholars in Bologna in 2001 as a nonprofit organization. The director is Dr. Enrico Marabini, a member of the Parapsychological Association. Paolo Presi is chief of the Voice Department and works with electronics engineer Daniele Gullà. The laboratory employs scientific methods and instruments to research and study "anomalous, unusual or nonconventional phenomena of 'psi interaction,' phenomena that depend on particular 'biopsychic conditions' and on bioresonance phenomena in which man has always been directly or indirectly involved."

Il Laboratorio defines biopsychocybernetics as involving phenomena caused by the influence of natural electromagnetic fields and geomagnetic and sidereal radiations on the human central nervous system and, as a consequence, on living systems—in other words, the energies of place and space on the mind, body, and consciousness of human beings. The laboratory takes an interdisciplinary approach to the interactions between human beings—physical and states of consciousness—and the influences of surrounding environments. Research is both practical, from investigations in the field, and theoretical.

Research falls into two broad camps: one examines the content of the messages, and one examines the process by which the messages happen. Presi has had a long interest in spirit communications and has followed the work of Bacci for years, examining the processes by which the spirits seem to communicate. He has overseen analyses of many paranormal voices produced in psychophonic, tele-phonic, and direct radio cases.

When direct radio voice research got under way in force in the 1970s, researchers assumed that the voices were being broadcast from the Beyond in a fashion similar to Earthside radio stations and that they could be heard by tuning into the right frequency with the right equipment. That model fell by the wayside. The experimenters—Bacci among them—discovered that voices come in on many frequencies over a variety of equipment. Radio voices speak more slowly than recorder voices, which are whispery and fast. In 1977 Carlo Trajna, the engineer who partici-pated in one of the Bacci experiments described earlier, argued that radios are not "receivers" of paranormal voices but are sonority generators that transform transmissions into "voices" by an unknown process.

The type and sophistication of the equipment often have little to do with the reception of voices and their quality. One device or radio works for one person and not another. As we have noted, the mediumistic ability of the experimenters has considerable influence. People who are critical and skeptical tend to have the worst results of all.

Il Laboratorio has demonstrated that paranormal

voices show an intent to communicate and therefore are not likely to be random sounds misinterpreted by listeners. Trajna demonstrated this in an analysis of paranormal messages compared to media advertisements. He analyzed the numbers of words in thousands of advertisements published in Italian newspapers and plotted them in an asymmetrical Gaussian curve. He took paranormal messages published by many leading researchers and found they followed a similar displacement. He did a second statistical analysis on the numbers of syllables in both the advertisements and the paranormal messages. According to the results, the paranormal messages show intention to communicate and are not mere distortions of sound.

Another important study, on speech identification, was conducted by Renato Orso in Turin. Orso took a sample of five paranormal messages and made a recording in which he repeated the messages himself. Both were analyzed by a sonograph. Results showed that the paranormal voices have an acoustical structure and speech rhythm similar to human voices. However, the paranormal voices lacked a fundamental frequency determined by the vibration of vocal cords. In other words, the paranormal voices were not coming from a human larynx. What this might mean, said Presi, is that an entity can interact with our physical dimension and "is able to overthrow known physical laws."

Paranormal voices differ from human voices by being higher or lower in speed. Sometimes words are compressed or phonemes are missing. In many cases, words seem to be formed from a "thickening" of the background noise. Presi has speculated that the unusual cadences and word structures might be caused by dilations and contractions in time flow, a process yet to be understood.

In 1990 Trajna developed a theoretical "psychotemporal model" in which psychic time flows differently from physical time. In this model, voices are caused by a psychotemporal wave activated by a discarnate entity, which shifts from subjective psychic time to objective physical time. The wave has four mathematically derived phases, three of which are "imaginary" and one of which is "real." The voices develop during the "real" phase. This could account for the brevity of most messages.

VOICE ANALYSIS

Il Laboratorio has employed sophisticated voice and image analysis software to EVP and Instrumental Transcommunication messages. These programs are used by agencies such as the Federal Bureau of Investigation to match voices and images for the purposes of identification.

One case cited by Presi involved voice messages obtained by Sonia Rinaldi of a girl named Edna, who had died at age sixteen when struck by a car. Rinaldi had the girl's adoptive mother, Cleusa, place a "phone call to the dead" on her laboratory setup. The conversation, in Portuguese, between Cleusa and Edna lasted fifteen minutes, during which Edna spoke seventy-eight times. While they were talking, three CDs containing phonemes in foreign languages other than Portuguese were played in the background. The sound mix was intended to aid communication, but the mix also meant that the production of meaningful sentences in Portuguese, especially related to the conversation, technically was impossible from the background noise alone, according to Presi. Yet the dead girl spoke comprehensible messages in Portuguese.

A single sentence spoken by the dead girl was sent to Il Laboratorio for analysis. Half of the sentence was modulated by the CD sounds, and half of it was free of sounds after the CDs were switched off. The second half was used for analysis.

Edna's paranormal voice was compared to her life voice using software called "FBI Image Searching," which performs both one-to-one matching and one-to-many matching. Il Laboratorio applied an acceptance limit of accuracy of greater than 95 percent.

In one-to-one, the two voices were compared with each other. The one-to-one match showed both were the same voice. In one-to-many, Edna's paranormal voice was compared to 909 voices in the database, 229 of which belonged to Brazilian speakers of Portuguese. A total of 48,600 calculations were performed over seven hours, and again, the two voices of the living and dead Edna matched.

The same software was used on a direct radio voice recorded in one of Bacci's sessions. The voice was that of Chiara Lenzi, the deceased daughter of Giuseppe Lenzi, a colleague of Bacci. Chiara communicated through Bacci's radio on several different occasions.

An analysis was done of her paranormal voice speaking one word: her name, Chiara. The FBI Image Searching software matched it to the voice of Chiara while living. In addition, Il Laboratorio recorded for comparison "Chiara" spoken individually by ten females ages sixteen to twenty who were living in Siena, Italy. Chiara had lived in Siena and thus had the same intonation and was in that age range when she died. Even with the addition of the Siena voices to the database, the software still matched the dead and living Chiara voices to each other.

In 2003 Chiara's voices were tested on signal-to-noise ratio using another software program called Idem, which had been designed for the Italian Magistracy and Italian Judicial Police for the identification of the voices of unknown speakers. The software analyzed vowels in a string of sentences spoken by her while alive against twenty seconds of her paranormal voice and compared them to a database of nine hundred voices. The match between Chiara's living and paranormal voices was greater than 99 percent.

In 2005 still another test was performed, when Chiara returned to communicate again. This time, she spoke her name and it registered only on one of four recorders that were operating (three were tape and one was digital)—the one held by her father. A spectrographic analysis showed that although there were some differences between her voice in the test and her voice when living, the two voices showed an "evident compatibility."

Researcher Anabela Cardoso had the voice of one of

her main Timestream communicators, Carlos de Almeida, analyzed by Il Laboratorio and also the Department of Acoustics at the University of Vigo; it was determined to have characteristics not typical of human voices.

Presi stressed that an absolute certainty of 100 percent cannot be achieved in voice matching because, unlike fingerprints, a person's voice can change and some people have remarkably similar voices to one another. Nonetheless, it is hard to ignore impressive results such as these. Are they proof that the dead have talked? The match possibilities are limited to the selections in the databases, but nonetheless, the software techniques are employed internationally in criminal, intelligence, legal, medical, and criminal matters. As Presi noted, the software is constantly improving in capability. There are versions of different programs available to the general public. Should more spirit communications researchers be using them? Compiling more data along these lines can only benefit the case for hard evidence.

13

No Love, No Light from the Dark Side

Sometimes contact with the spirit world brings more than a person bargains for. Not all entities who are able to communicate across dimensions have good intentions.

Manfred Boden was a German cabinetmaker who was minding his own business when the spirit world intruded with a nasty message typed out without explanation on his computer screen: he was going to die. The message, allegedly sent to him by a dead person he knew, hurled him into a tailspin of fear and anxiety that intensified as the predicted death date drew nearer. He had nearly two years to worry.

Fortunately for Boden, the case had a happy ending,

though it left psychological scars. Boden was by no means alone in unpleasant dealings with the spirit realm. Plenty of other people have had run-ins with dark forces. While spirit communications researchers emphasize the love, the light, and the high morals and ethics, there is a black underbelly that must be dealt with.

Not every entity who reaches out from the Beyond is friendly. Hostile communications have been a hazard of spirit contact from the beginning, and as we have already seen, the spirits are sometimes full of pranks. The lower astral realms are said to be inhabited by malicious dead people and entities masquerading as the dead or other higher beings. They are all opportunistic when a channel opens—and they are not nice. It is not uncommon for them to utter "kill" threats or make dire predictions that someone listening is going to die. The purpose of these messages is to frighten and intimidate. This type of experience is often reported by individuals who play with talking boards, but threats also come over devices such as the ghost boxes and through direct voice radio.

The Boden case took place in 1980. It may have been the first case—or at least the first known case—in which computers were used in such a manner by an alleged spirit.

At the time, Boden was not involved in paranormal research and contacting the dead was not on his agenda. On December 10 of that year, he was working with a colleague, Juergen, and entered the text of a biorhythm program on his computer. Mysteriously, Boden's first and last name appeared on the screen, plus the name of an acquaintance who had died about three months prior and who was known to both Boden and Juergen. Then an ominous sentence appeared: "I am here, you will die, Manfred, 1982 accident August 16, 1982. Yours, Klaus."

Another mystery text appeared later on Boden's computer announcing: "HEART ATTACK, HI HI." The messages were alarming to Boden, who was a nervous, overweight chain-smoker and heavy drinker. As the day of his forecasted death approached, he grew more anxious and sought out the help and advice of experts, including researchers Ernst Senkowski, Ralf Determeyer, and Guenter Heim.

Senkowski assured Boden that no deceased person would ever terrify a living friend in such a manner and therefore the message must be from a deceitful imposter. He called the messages "seemingly soulless." Still, Boden was quite distraught. Who would not be scared under the circumstances? Throughout history, humans have consulted the dead about the future and have given great weight to spirit pronouncements about impending events, believing the spirits to be able to see futures the living cannot. And we get powerful reinforcement from films and fiction, which use spirit warnings of death followed by actual death as plot devices in horror stories.

How could Boden know for certain the messages were a trick? Was it worth the risk to ignore them?

Boden's forecasted death date came and went without incident. Even so, Boden remained a bundle of nerves for some time. Senkowski concluded the episode was para-normal; Boden had a hard time coming to terms with how it all happened. He died in 1990.

The psychological toll on Boden demonstrates the very real danger of such spirit threats, even if they are empty. British psychiatrist J. C. Barker, who was a member of the Society for Psychical Research, wrote on the deadly effects of fear in his book *Scared to Death* (1968). He examined the effects of fortune-telling death predictions and concluded that it is possible for people who are sufficiently frightened by news of impending death to literally scare themselves to death exactly as predicted, including the time and manner, thus fulfilling the prophecy. Barker speculated a type of psychokinetic force might be unleashed in such cases. We cannot overemphasize the importance of being well grounded before attempting any kind of spirit communications and that one's motives should never be for entertainment or thrills.

But can the proverbial bad things still happen to good people? Are researchers and experimenters who are well grounded and well intentioned in any danger from hostile entities who can strike out through spirit contact?

The researchers working with Timestream and other transcommunication groups in the 1980s did have problems. Oddly, negative entities often identified themselves as groups whose names were numbers. Technician acknowledged that hostile entities were trying to take over the transmitting stations and disrupt communications and also mentally influence researchers who did not have the right mental preparation for the work. In 1986 Konstantin Raudive warned in a phone message, "There are many cases in which mystics and adepts are bodily and especially mentally harmed in spite of observing all the rules . . ."

The warning may have been a heads-up for what was coming. There were various problems from malicious sources. In 1987 a negative group called Group 2105 purportedly captured the Timestream transmitting station on the astral plane and disrupted communications. It had to be recaptured, giving the incident the appearance of an all-too-familiar earthly war scenario.

The Harsch-Fischbach couple began receiving transmissions on their computer from a Group 2405 but terminated the link when it seemed that the entities did not have positive spiritual attitudes. Other researchers were beset by problems, including health issues, relationship and professional issues, projects that failed, and even other spirit threats of death. One of the researchers who worked with the spirit group called ABX Juno, contracted throat cancer (which ultimately caused his death), a tragedy that made others wonder if it might have been related to his spirit communications work. Kenneth Webster, an English teacher, received via his computer a "senseless" poem signed by "Group 2109." The group wanted to work with him, but he did not like their cold "feel" and declined. Mark Macy had phone messages from an entity masquerading as Raudive, who spoke in a "demonic" voice.

The spirit interference exacerbated the personal turmoil that developed among researchers and according to some opinions may have even caused the turmoil. Some of the spirits were open in their hostility while others were crafty and disguised. The Harsch-Fischbach couple even stopped their experiments and lectures for several weeks in an effort to disengage the negative forces—plus, they felt they needed a break from the demands for information that were piling up.

Maggy Harsch-Fischbach made no attempt to hide or minimize the problems caused by negative spirits, believing that everyone who enters the field should be aware of the dangers in it in order to be able to master fear. "To think that one would never encounter a negative entity is the same as expecting to meet only perfect people in this life," she said in *Breakthroughs in Technical Spirit Communication*, co-authored with Dr. Theo Locher (1997). She also said that a negative entity is not always a low-vibration entity, for every being, good or bad, is subject to engaging in negative thoughts and activities. Not every spirit in the Beyond likes spirit communications experimenters and their work. "Some of them loathe friendship and unity among man for a special reason," she said. "They do not like the Light."

VULNERABILITY OF THE GRIEVING

People who have lost loved ones and turn to Electronic Voice Phenomena as part of their grief processing can become targets for malicious spirits. Senkowski warned: "We must here point out a great danger many are not aware of. Any spirit can pretend to be the one they look for! They can telepathically tap the mind of any living human and provide any answer the experimenter is looking for. This may result in blind trust and great psychological entanglement of the experimenter."

EXTRATERRESTRIALS OR A MASQUERADE?

Friedrich Jürgenson became convinced for a time that the spirit communicators talking to him were extraterrestrials. His wife thought so, too. There were references to friends from space, ships, and radar. In 1959 he became so immersed in "voices from nowhere" that he began to doubt his own sanity and worried about schizophrenia.

In the late 1950s, public interest in UFOs and ETs was high. Thousands of sightings of lights and craft were being reported all over the world. It made sense to Jürgenson that the voices of a pair of male and female communicators were those of a UFO crew. He and his wife became "hooked," he said, on the popular ideology that the ETs were here to save humanity from itself. At their forest cottage in Mölnbo, Sweden, Jürgenson had intense experiences with voices emanating from the air around him and in background noises.

Ultimately, he said, he and wife suddenly felt they had been strung along, "betrayed and mocked by these unknown entities," as he put it. They felt deeply ashamed of their gullibility. In his book *Voice Transmissions with the Deceased*, Jürgenson wrote:

I can still remember that in the very moment when I had enough, and then placed my finger on the "off"-switch, I could clearly hear these words of a male voice in my headphones: "Please wait—wait—listen to us . . ." But I didn't wait and I didn't listen anymore either. Instead I closed the lid on my reel-to-reel, gathered all my tapes, and was determined to radically call it "quits" with this nonsense.

I was bitter beyond compare and placed the entire blame for this avoidable fiasco with these "spirits" that had made a fool of all of us.

We quickly packed our belongings, locked up the cottage and the large house by the lake, and drove back to Stockholm. I felt somehow relieved, though our departure could have been compared to fleeing.

Jürgenson was so distraught over being duped by tricky communicators that he put away his recorder and wanted no more to do with Electronic Voice Phenomena. One day weeks later he was in his studio listening to the sound of rain outside when the same familiar female voice emerged out of the rain noise and urged him to hold contact with his equipment daily. "Please, please listen," she said. The voice spoke the same message out of the sound of rustling paper, the crackling of fire in the stove, and the buzz of his electric razor as he shaved. He felt nervous and tense and took up smoking. His hearing became increasingly acute. After the passage of more time, he became more relaxed. Then one day a male voice spoke in the air around him, saying, "Listen to me: take part in the work." Jürgenson felt ready to resume his experiments, and he got out his tape recorder and started taping voices again. If he ever solved the mystery of the alleged "space friends," he did not say.

A PERSISTENT HAZARD

There is scarcely a paranormal investigator or spirit communications researcher who has *not* had a negative experience from communicators. Sometimes a negative spirit will start in with obscenities, insults, and threats. Rosemary even had one that voiced his dislike perhaps for the whole spirit communications field by saying, "Hate the box, hate the box," when she turned on her MiniBox. If a communicator becomes abusive, she tells it to go away, and if it does not stop, she ends the session and turns off the box. Other researchers do the same—terminate a session if necessary.

However, some worry that unpleasant entities may linger Earthside even after a session is terminated. Is it possible? We can't rule out the possibility, and researchers are divided on the topic. Some, like Ron Ricketts, the designer of the MiniBox, feel that once a session is over the communicators are shut off. "The box is a medium and has to be activated to be the medium of exchange," he said. "When you turn on the box a psychic link is formed and it stays until you turn it off. The power of the switch is the ultimate finality—when you turn it off the box dies and whatever is there dies with it."

Margaret Downey, who works with the grieving, reports no negative experiences herself and attributes that to her positive orientation and the protection of spirit guides with whom she works. "I have a deep trust in my spirit team, and they are not going to let something negative come through," she said. Once she did get a voice that emanated from a closet that said, in classic Hollywood horror film fashion, "*Get out!*" "I thought it was a kid or teen on the Other Side playing a prank—not a demon," Margaret said. "I do think there are some who like to play jokes."

The communicators, she said, will mold themselves to whatever the experimenters feel is necessary in terms of opening and closing sessions. "Those on the Other Side are extremely accommodating to our beliefs," she said. "If we need them to tell us the portal is shut to close the session, they will accommodate that. I don't feel any spirit or entity gets stuck on this side after a session. I am the instrument, not the other way around. If I close the session and my energetic system, no one is left stuck. It's like shutting my front door with someone standing on the other side—they are not stuck or locked in the house with me."

Likewise, on the few occasions when negative communicators have manifested during sessions Rosemary has conducted nothing has remained behind. The key may be fear. Those of us who plumb the paranormal depths in any area quickly learn that we attract presences with our thoughts and emotions. A person who fears attachments will *attract* attaching entities. Some people seem to be naturally sticky, and spirits and energies adhere to them. It is important for those who wish to engage in spirit communications to know their inner self, be well grounded, and have some study of the field under their belts. Technician once told Maggy that certain equipment should be built only by a person who has a "well-integrated personality."

REMEDIES AND PROTECTION

There probably is not anything that can be done to completely prevent negative encounters, but they can be minimized. The pursuit of a spiritual life is central to protection. Praying and meditating, coupled with adhering to one's spiritual principles and faith, cultivating a positive mental attitude, following high ethical standards, and maintaining harmony and balance in daily life, are important. A person's thoughts, emotions, actions, and overall spiritual energy can be seen and sensed by other entities on the spiritual planes. They are drawn to us accordingly. Like attracts like.

While all of these strengthen a person's aura and spiritual armor, they won't necessarily stop a negative entity from having a go. Some people think—and naïvely so—that informing the spirits that they only want to talk to "good" ones or to "beings of love and light" will guarantee that the bad ones won't get past the gate. As we have seen, disguises and masquerades are possible. Senkowski cautioned against the gullibility of some researchers whose wishful thinking for certain results could be used against them by deceitful spirits.

A POSTSCRIPT ON MANFRED BODEN

Boden's involvement in spirit communications did not end with his empty death forecast. He tried experimenting with Electronic Voice Phenomena on tape and was successful right away. Apparently, Boden had latent psychic and mediumistic ability—but apparently, he also did not have a good personality for engaging in spirit communications. He was looking for "harmless entertainment," but he attracted more trouble.

The EVP voices told him they would start communicating by phone, which they did, from 1981 to 1983. The spirits were not malicious, but they were tricksters and they unleashed annoying pranks and phenomena upon him and others he talked to on the phone, especially his friend Juergen and his girlfriend Ursula. Sometimes Boden's phone conversations would be interrupted and pushed off the line by an unknown entity, who then communicated with Boden by answering his questions in a yes or no fashion by making clicking sounds.

Sometimes unknown voices speaking German, French, and English interrupted his phone conversations and then answered his questions. Strangely—or perhaps not— Ursula could not hear the voices. The entities told Boden the reason she could not was because she was not psychic. Sometimes he telepathically received the answers to his questions before he asked them.

The new communicators were polite and described themselves as "energy beings." They admonished Boden not to drink so much.

Boden began to hear from dead people by phone, some of whom identified themselves as former members of his ham radio club. However, they spoke in jumbled sentences that made no sense, just like a trickster might do. Dead relatives called to harangue him with religious messages. There were other voices as well, often anonymous phone callers who rang late into the night. Boden made many recordings of his calls. Poltergeist phenomena erupted in his home, including mysterious disappearances of objects, the tilting of empty bottles, and other events. Boden's nervous anxiety increased.

Ursula and Juergen began to be affected as well. In early 1983, Boden's relationship with Ursula was winding down. She accused him of calling her late at night, awakening her, to breathe heavily into the phone. At the same time, he was getting calls from someone who sounded like Ursula. Neither of them placed the calls to each other. Juergen complained of problems with weird phone calls and difficulties with his computer. He feared others would think he was crazy. Juergen remained upset for years and as a result wanted to distance himself as much as possible from the paranormal. Ursula, meanwhile, became engaged in the practice of magic.

In May and June of 1984, Boden had phone calls with two living people during which a constant noise like a generator buzzed in the background. The noise went quiet when he spoke and started up whenever he stopped. The others could not hear it, only Boden.

Then something truly scary started happening: wishes made during calls came true instantly, but in bizarre ways. Boden could ask callers for wishes and they would manifest. Once he asked a friend, Gerd, to make a wish over the phone, and suggested he ask for music of the spheres. Immediately there was music accompanied by the sounds of rushing water and cuckoo calls (a nice Trickster touch). Boden asked for more cuckoo calls and got three and then five in response. Gerd heard nothing. Boden then wished for more drastic spirit manifestations as proof that the spirits were causing these things. Immediately in Gerd's home, objects smashed to the floor: flowers, audiocassettes, a picture, and other items. A flying flowerpot smacked him in the head. After that, Gerd avoided contact with Boden.

The progression of events here follows a typical Trickster format. First there is the death prediction that is false. Fear ensues, then is replaced by curiosity and a desire to be entertained. The new voices are friendly and polite, give themselves a high spiritual pedigree, and cause interesting but minimal disturbances. Then the disturbances become darker and more disruptive and affect others as well, causing mental and emotional turmoil. In Boden's case, there seemed to be an absence of threatening voices (often a characteristic of deteriorating spirit contact), but the phenomena became more destructive.

It is all too easy to get caught in a downward spiral like this if one engages in spirit communications for the wrong reasons, such as entertainment, and lacks preparation. The only ones truly entertained are the time-wasting beings on the other end.

Fortunately, problems comprise a very small part of spirit communications. It is best, however, to be aware of pitfalls in order to avoid them.

14

Skeptics and the Afterlife

One night on Open Lines we brought up the topic of spirit communications and a caller named Mike commented that he was opposed to the research.

"Don't you want to know what happens to us after we die?" I asked.

"I already know," he replied. "The Bible makes it very clear. I don't need to know anything else. These researchers who say they are talking to the dead—it's all the Devil's work. They're being fooled."

Rosemary, who was with me in the studio that night, chimed in, "There are a lot of people who feel like Mike— they have definite beliefs about the afterlife based on their religious teachings, and they feel that it is not right, even dangerous, to challenge those beliefs."

"Isn't progress *about* challenging the status quo?" I asked.

"We absolutely must explore the evidence for the afterlife," she said. "It's clear that spirits and the dead have been talking to us since ancient times—and that we want to talk to them, too. We certainly keep trying! Technology is giving us better and more reliable ways to do that. But yes, there is a very good possibility that we will learn things about death and the afterlife that conflict with many beliefs held by people now."

"We've talked many times about the people who are inventing devices and ways to communicate with the Other Side," I said. "Why doesn't science participate more?"

"There are a few scientists and people with hard science backgrounds who are interested in spirit communications," she said. "But by and large, science steers clear of it and the paranormal in general. The paranormal just doesn't conform to scientific standards for research. We've seen that in psychical research and parapsychology."

"Are we really afraid to know what's out there?" I wondered.

"I think that's a good part of it," Rosemary said.

"Let's explore this a little more," I said, inviting caller response. "Should we keep searching for proof of the afterlife?"

After the commercial break, a woman named Cathy was on the line. "I'm listening to what you're talking about, and I'm one of those who really don't want to know," she confessed. "I mean, I believe that after we die we go somewhere. But that's it."

"You don't want to know the details of where you go and what you'll be doing?" I asked.

"I guess it's something I don't want to think about right now," she said.

"Do you think we go to a good place when we die?"

"Well, yes. But how do we really know what to believe?"

"It's true there are many different accounts of the afterlife, and not all of them agree," Rosemary said. "That's one of the reasons why I think it's important for us to pursue this research, to get proof and validation."

Another caller advocated spirit communications research for personal reasons. "My grandpa died about four months ago," said a woman named Megan. "I really miss him. I'd really like to know for sure that he's okay. I wish there was a way for me to talk to him—I'd use it!"

"I've lost both my parents," Rosemary said. "I would love to talk to them, too, especially my dad. We were both amateur astronomers, and I'd like to find out if he ever got answers to any of his questions about the cosmos."

We took more calls, and listeners remained divided on the subject of whether or not it's a good idea to look for proof of the afterlife, especially by talking to the dead. Most callers favored research for a variety of reasons, but there seem to be many out there who do not—or at least they fear finding out facts that will force them to reexamine their beliefs.

We decided to investigate the reluctance to know and the outright disbelief in spirit communications and the afterlife. We were surprised at some of our findings concerning who is on what side of the coin.

PARAPSYCHOLOGY

The most obvious field that should take a strong interest in spirit communications and the afterlife is parapsychology, which evolved out of psychical research. By the mid-twentieth century, researchers had mostly abandoned studies of mediumship, which had not produced the proof scientists were looking for. Parapsychologists retreated to the laboratory to concentrate on statistical research on the performance of psi (extrasensory perception and telepathy) and psychokinesis, or PK (the influence of thought and intention over matter). By the turn of the twenty-first century, interest in survival-after-death research risked a kiss of professional death, not to mention the inability to obtain research grants.

A few parapsychologists paid attention to spirit communications. Jürgenson's work attracted the attention of Prof. Hans Bender, founder of the Institute for Frontier Areas of Psychology and Mental Health in Freiburg, Germany. Bender, who became a towering figure in parapsychology, at first was convinced that EVP voices did not belong to the dead but were manifestations of thoughts in the subconscious of Jürgenson and others who participated in the sessions. Somehow the thoughts became impressed on tape through projection. This psychokinesis could be unwitting, Bender said, leading experimenters to think their results were coming from the dead.

To his credit, Bender continued his research, inviting Jürgenson to Germany to conduct more experiments. Bender also became involved with Raudive. Bender's fascination with Electronic Voice Phenomena led him to become one of the leading researchers of it in the world. He kept an open mind and soon came to believe that the voices did come from the dead, after all. (Bender is now the main spirit contact for a materialization group called Felix Experimental Group in Germany.)

Raudive made trips to England to demonstrate Electronic Voice Phenomena to skeptics. He was unprepared for the controversy that erupted over his work. People were polarized, either predisposed to belief or predisposed to disbelief. Some of the strongest disbelievers and critics were members of the British parapsychological community the Society for Psychical Research. The media attention was intense.

In 1970 Raudive accepted a challenge by a Cambridge University student, David Ellis. Ellis believed that Raudive's Electronic Voice Phenomena were normal foreign radio transmissions. He proposed to conduct experiments with a reel-to-reel tape recorder placed inside a Faraday cage, which is made of copper and screens out external radio signals. If the voices were not coming from radio transmissions, then they would be recorded. The experiment was not a wild success. Only one voice was recorded, and Ellis concluded it was external noise that sounded like a voice.

In 1971 Raudive went back to England at the invitation of Pye Records, which offered him their state-of-the-art recording equipment in their soundproof and shielded London studio. Raudive produced numerous voices, many of which could not be explained naturally. Voices identified themselves as dead persons and said they were calling attention to themselves—they wanted to be noticed. British scientists and parapsychologists remained unimpressed. The voices, some critics said, were too obscure and the messages too short to be of any real and convincing value. And while many members of the public seemed persuaded by the evidence, no great turning of public opinion about proof of an afterlife happened.

Other EVP researchers ran into more stone walls. George Gilbert Bonner, an English psychologist and artist, was inspired by Raudive. Over the next twenty-two years, Bonner, using white noise, recorded more than fifty thousand voices—but still could not get the interest of scientists or parapsychologists.

Raymond Cass, a consultant on hearing aids, recorded thousands of EVP voices. On August 23, 1976, Cass received a startling message on his battery-operated tape recorder, used in conjunction with a multiband radio tuned to the air band. The hoarse voice that literally shouted out was the unmistakable, distinctive voice of Raudive, who had died in 1974. Raudive said in German, "Here's Raudive . . . waiting at the bridge!"

The message evoked a vivid picture of an eager researcher standing at a meeting point beyond which he could go no farther, waiting for the living to see the bridge and cross it. He was waiting, waiting, waiting—and what was the problem on the other end? Technology? Attitude? A lack of belief?

Tens of thousands of compelling recordings that defy explanation have been documented since those early days, but many parapsychologists still dismiss Electronic Voice Phenomena. Their most common objections are that Electronic Voice Phenomena are misinterpreted but natural radio voices or stray radio signals and that listeners are hearing words that are not there but are imagined. The brain does have a natural tendency to make patterns and sense out of our sensory experiences. Misjudging Electronic Voice Phenomena is a hazard acknowledged by all researchers. Especially vulnerable, they say, are grieving people and those overeager to make contact with the dead.

Most of the research that goes on today is done quietly by private interests. Gone for the most part are the attempts to demonstrate evidence to the media and the general public. But don't be fooled—the amount of research, innovation, and experimentation is considerable, all over the planet.

The ATransC has advocated more scientific research. "We can pretty well prove that Electronic Voice Phenomena are producing phenomenal voices," co-director Tom Butler told us. "It's an easily reproduced experiment." But some of the methods used to capture voices, especially real-time, have their hazards. Radio sweep, said Butler, is vulnerable to misinterpretation—"storytelling," as he calls it, the tendency to hear what we want to hear.

Software such as EVPMaker, which uses fragments of human speech, produces more reliable results in the eyes of many—but even that has its issues with "false positives," or mistaken communications. Kristian Tigersjal, an EVP researcher in Orebro, Sweden, coined the term "Electronic Noise Phenomena," or "ENP," to describe misinterpreted noise. Random noise can be "heard" as voices by a process known as pareidolia, a natural tendency of the brain to search for meaning in random patterns. Pareidolia can account for the tendency to see faces in clouds and background foliage, for example. It has also been advanced as an explanation for Electronic Voice Phenomena—or at least some of the messages we think we are getting. We hear a jumble of sound and pick out voices from it.

ENP can happen without a person being aware of it. Low sounds in a background, such as the soft noise of rushing water, can easily produce "voices." So can many small digital recorders that record compressed files such as MP3 and WMA, especially when used at their lowest settings; there is an internal noise that can be misconstrued as faint voices. Furthermore, manipulation of files with audio software—even if well-intentioned to boost a faint "voice"—can sometimes create voices or make what seem to be voices pop out of the background noise. The result is a created Electronic Voice Phenomenon, not an enhanced Electronic Voice Phenomenon.

Researchers have done studies to determine how likely "storytelling" is. Results have fallen on both sides, showing misinterpretations and also showing the opposite. The ATransC was a sponsor of a study on radio sweep conducted in partnership with the Windbridge Institute for Applied Research in Human Potential, an independent scientific-research organization in Tucson that studies survival of consciousness (mostly involving mediums), alternative healing, and applied intuition. (The institute was founded by Mark Boccuzzi and Julie Beischel; Beischel worked with Gary Schwartz's study of mediumship in his former VERITAS program at the University of Arizona at Tucson.)

The ATransC took a sample of radio sweep Electronic Voice Phenomena, posted it online, and invited responses of interpretations. Forty-one people responded, with widely varying interpretations. Butler's report on the radio sweep study, released in 2010, concluded that radio sweep does not produce empirical, or hard, evidence of Electronic Voice Phenomena.

Nonetheless, opinions of researchers diverge sharply, not only on radio sweep but on all methods of obtaining Electronic Voice Phenomena. Philip Imbrogno has analyzed many of the EVP communications. Initially, Phil was skeptical of radio sweep boxes; then he became convinced that genuine real-time Electronic Voice Phenomena can come through them, probably when an interdimensional portal opens in the Earth's magnetosphere. "The Electronic Voice Phenomenon seems to be a very weak signal that piggybacks onto the stronger signal of the radio," he said.

"The Electronic Voice Phenomena are not part of the terrestrial radio broadcasts. They are a separate transmission and seem to be produced by intelligent design." Radio sweep has its limitations and drawbacks, Phil acknowledged. "It may not be the most efficient way to obtain real-time Electronic Voice Phenomena, but we can't dismiss it out of hand."

Rosemary remains a firm supporter of radio sweep: "Presently we have *no* method of collecting Electronic Voice Phenomena that is foolproof and that meets scientific standards. Our technology for interdimensional contact is still primitive. We have to keep all doors open. I have gotten too many communications via radio sweep that cannot be explained naturally."

Electronic Voice Phenomena, as well as psychic phenomena, seldom fit into neat scientific molds. No wonder many scientists shy away from spirit communications.

SCIENCE

For some scientists, explaining Electronic Voice Phenomena is easy—it is all a fallacy, because there is no proof of survival of consciousness. The eminent Harvard psychologist Steven Pinker stated in his article in *TIME* magazine (2004):

And when the physiological activity of the brain ceases, as far as anyone can tell the person's consciousness goes out of existence. Attempts to contact the souls of the dead (a pursuit of serious scientists a century ago) turned up only cheap magic tricks, and near death experiences are not the eyewitness reports of a soul parting company from the body but symptoms of oxygen starvation in the eyes and brain.

There have been exposures of fraud in the history of mediumship, just as in any field. However, a century-plus of survival research by serious scientists has amassed impressive evidence that, while not scientific proof, is difficult to explain away. We probably do not know everything there is to know about human consciousness—we have probably barely scratched the surface—so it is problematic to make definitive statements about whether or not consciousness survives death. Most of the planet's population has always believed in some form of survival of consciousness and perhaps even personality. Is it wishful thinking out of fear of annihilation? Is it solely an article of faith, a tool of religion for control? Or is it based on a long history of subjective experience that convinces us that another life awaits us beyond the body? Whatever the reasons, science is not going to eradicate belief in an afterlife. Instead, science should be *pursuing* evidence of survival.

Jürgenson made the following observation in *Voice Transmissions with the Deceased:*

It is a fact that there still exist researchers in our day and age who would rather credit my subconscious with the most absurd magic tricks than to admit honestly and courageously the proven fact that the human personality survives after death in another dimension. If these researchers had only paid attention to other possible insights rather than to the excessive cultivation of their own intellect, they would gain the courage and insights necessary to revise their obsolete views of the world and mankind. How much damage has already been wrought in our world by ideologies built on cold intellect alone!

Most scientists shy away from studying the evidence for survival, according to David Fontana, a psychologist, who was a survival research expert and former president of the Society for Psychical Research in England. Instead, they refute it, usually on the grounds that no good studies have been done. Some critics have not examined the studies that have been done, but consider these studies as flawed.

According to Fontana, "The main reason for this uninformed hostility on the part of many scientists toward psychical research is the belief that if psychic abilities exist and if the mind survives death (and is therefore nonphysical), many of the most fundamental laws of science would have to be rewritten. This claim is of course absurd." Instead, Fontana said, scientists fear that if survival is true, it challenges the supremacy of material science, reducing it from the ultimate authority on life, death, and everything to simply the science of material things.

RELIGION

Religious reactions to Electronic Voice Phenomena encompass pro, con, and neutral stances and, unfortunately, threats against researchers. Interestingly, the Catholic Church, which centuries ago instigated the Inquisition, has been the most tolerant and open.

In 1952 two Catholic priests, had an astonishing and unexpected episode of Electronic Voice Phenomena. Fr. Agostino Gemelli of Italy was a medical laureate, psychologist, and neurophysiologist, a member of the Grey Friars, and interested in the psychology of the workplace. Fr. Pellegrino Ernetti was an Italian Roman Catholic Benedictine priest, a scientist, and an authority on archaic music, pre-Christian to the tenth century. Gemelli was a founder of the Catholic University of the Sacred Heart of Milan, where both men collaborated on music research that included using electronic equipment to improve the quality of recorded singing voices. Perhaps a factor in their surprising Electronic Voice Phenomena was Gemelli's longtime habit of calling upon his dead father for help whenever he had a problem. He never received a direct answer, but situations always seemed to sort themselves out when he did so.

On September 15, 1952, Gemelli and Ernetti were recording a Gregorian chant on magnetic tape. A wire in their tape recorder kept breaking. Exasperated, Gemelli kept fixing it, finally calling upon his father for help. Recorded on the tape was his voice saying in response, "Of course I shall help you. I'm always with you."

The priests were shocked and immediately thought it was a deception of the Devil. But Ernetti urged trying to get the voice again. They recorded the same voice saying, with a humorous tone, "But, Zucchini, it is clear; don't you know it is I?"

For Gemelli, the shock deepened. No one—literally *no one*—knew his boyhood nickname, which his father had always used when teasing him. Certain it was his father speaking, Gemelli could not help but feel joyful. But then his religious training overshadowed his joy: did he have a right to speak with the dead?

Some time later, Gemelli and Ernetti had an audience with Pope Pius XII (pope from 1939 to 1958) in Rome. Gemelli was still deeply troubled by his experience and shared it with the pope. To Gemelli's amazement, Pius XII was not at all disturbed. "Dear Father Gemelli, you really need not worry about this," he assured the priest. "This existence of this voice is strictly a scientific fact, and has nothing whatsoever to do with spiritism. This recorder is totally objective. It receives and records only sound waves from wherever they come. This experiment may perhaps become the cornerstone for a building for scientific studies which will strengthen people's faith in a hereafter."

The pope's words only partially eased Gemelli's anxiety, however, and he said little about the incident until near the end of his life; he died in 1959 in Milan. Ernetti was more open about it and enjoyed debating the incident and its implications with others.

It is not surprising that Pius XII was open-minded about the spirit voice, for he was broad-minded about the spirit realm in general. At a time when popular belief in angels was at a low, he was a strong champion of them and said in a 1950 encyclical that it is a mistake not to think of them as real beings. He urged people to pray to their guardian angel.

A cousin of Pius XII, Gebhard Frei, was a parapsychologist of international repute. Frei was a co-founder of the Jung Institute and president of the International Society for Catholic Parapsychologists. He worked with Raudive and stated that the evidence convinced him that the voices were transcendental. Whether it suited him or not, he had no right to doubt the reality of them, he said. In 1970 the society devoted time to consideration of Electronic Voice Phenomena at its international conference.

Pope Paul VI (pope from 1963 to 1978), supported Jürgenson, primarily because of his film work and his documentary of the pope, and even made him a Knight Commander of the Order of St. Gregory in 1969. However, the pontiff knew about Jürgenson's EVP research. Jürgenson told Peter Bander that he had found a "sympathetic ear" at the Vatican and had "won many wonderful friends among the leading figures in the Holy City."

The Vatican also gave permission to some priests to conduct their own EVP research and has supported other parapsychological research.

In 1987 Fr. François Brune sat in the Harsch-Fischbach home in Luxembourg and heard the voices of Raudive and

Technician addressing him personally in French. Brune, a member of the Catholic Institute in Paris and the Biblical Institute in Rome, went on to write a book about Electronic Voice Phenomena, *Les Morts nous parlent* (*The Dead Speak to Us*), and to stimulate interest in EVP research in France. He also went on to become an international authority in the field. Brune said transcommunication will help prepare humanity for further spiritual evolution and is a gift from God that is needed for faith.

By the turn of the twenty-first century, Brune had collected thousands of EVP voices from all over the world, mostly by using a tape recorder and a microphone. He said he had no doubt about survival after death.

In 1997 Fr. Gino Concetti, a leading Vatican theologian, issued this statement, which supports communication with the dead under the proper conditions:

> According to the modern catechism, God allows our dear departed persons who live in an ultra-terrestrial dimension, to send messages to guide us in certain difficult moments of our lives. The Church has decided not to forbid anymore the dialogue with the deceased with the condition that these contacts are carried out with a serious religious and scientific purpose.

In May 2008, Fr. José Gabriel Funes, the Vatican's top astronomer, issued a statement acknowledging the possibility of alien life-forms and stating that believing in them is not contradictory to having faith in God. While the statement did not directly address the afterlife and spirit communicators, it could certainly be given a broad interpretation to include them.

Funes said aliens are still creatures of God. He then made a statement worthy of note. "The Bible is not a science book."

Funes also urged the church and the scientific community to heal the rift caused by Galileo's persecution. (To his credit, Pope John Paul had said earlier, in 1992, that the ruling against Galileo was an error resulting from "tragic mutual incomprehension.")

In early years of Electronic Voice Phenomena, efforts were made to demonstrate tests to religious authorities. Bander, for example, invited four Catholic authorities to the Pye recording studio tests. One of them, Father Pistone, Superior of the Society of St Paul in England, said afterward that he saw no reason to fear the voices or that there was anything in Electronic Voice Phenomena that contradicted the teachings of the church.

Over time, most religious organizations have taken scant official interest in Electronic Voice Phenomena and spirit communications. Tom and Lisa Butler, the directors of the ATransC since 2000, report very little contact with religious leaders, even on a local level. The Butlers are Spiritualists.

Some conservative fundamentalists are vocal about their opposition to Electronic Voice Phenomena and spirit communications and do use the Bible as a science book. They claim that if God wanted the living to talk to the dead, he would have provided the means to do so. Others claim the voices are masquerading demons, not the dead. Apparently, such individuals think that *all* beliefs about the afterlife should conform to whatever *their* particular religion of choice teaches them. Research that is contradictory threatens their belief systems.

Opponents to the field cite Bible verses such as Ecclesiastes 9:5: "For the living know that they will die, but the dead know nothing, and they have no more reward, for the memory of them is forgotten"; and Psalms 146:3, which states that when "mere man" dies "he returns to the dust; in that very day his thoughts perish."

There are no dead people to talk to the living, they say, because the dead are sleeping until the Second Coming, when they will have a resurrection of the body. But even with the resurrection of the body, there follows a judgment and an afterlife, according to Romans 2:6–11. The righteous will be rewarded with eternal life in a glorified body, and the wicked will be punished with wrath and anger.

"I occasionally get flack from religious people," said Margaret Downey. "What astounds me is, they don't stop to ask anything about Electronic Voice Phenomena or how it happens—they immediately assume that evil demons are trying to trick me."

Some of the researchers we interviewed for this book acknowledged being harassed and threatened by fundamentalists, but they did not wish to speak on the record about it. They have been called "servants of Satan" and accused of doing "the Devil's work" or "going against God." Some have had threats made against members of their families. The worst offenders are self-appointed inquisitors who hide behind anonymity on the Internet. This opposition is not likely to go away but may become worse as the evidence improves.

THE PUBLIC

As we have seen, not everyone is enthusiastic about penetrating into the Other Side. Some say the evidence seems too good to be true, while others retreat to their religious views. Still others are momentarily fascinated but then become uncertain about what to believe. Media coverage is often nonexistent or mocking and derisive.

Modern insulation from the reality of death may be a reason why the general public has yet to embrace survival research. Advances in health care and an emphasis on youth and materialism in the industrialized West have led to resistance to discussing death and the afterlife. In times past, people often died at home and were prepared there for burial, so there was no escaping dealing with death. Today, people are more likely to die in a health-care institution and be whisked straightaway to a funeral home.

Aversion and disinterest cannot last in the long run, however, for at some point we are likely to be confronted with evidence we cannot afford to ignore, much like the scenarios ufologists envision when we finally come face-to-face with alien life-forms.

The public will have to be reeducated, probably slowly in order to avoid major upsets. Jürgenson believed that the spirit communicators themselves are slowly acclimatizing us in order to avoid sudden shock. "I have often asked myself what would happen if the voices of well-known deceased personalities like Einstein, Pope Pius XII, Annie Besant, Hitler, Stalin, Count Ciano, Caruso, etc., were suddenly to be heard full force on the radio," he said. "Probably this would lead to general confusion and reactions of shock. It is also possible that East and West would accuse each other of provocative actions and that science and religion would also chime in. Without a slow, rational preparation of the general public it would all lead to misunderstanding, damage and contestation, eventually remaining as an unsolved puzzle that would heat up popular emotions just like the UFO's."

Human beings do seem ill equipped for radical shifts in worldviews. We have seen a similar scenario in ET contact and ufology—tantalizing anecdotal evidence of contact but no hard proof, and scientific unwillingness to delve into the action.

However, we no longer have the luxury of slower-paced change as we did in centuries past. Technology is hurtling us through all manner of changes at faster and faster speeds. When we are eventually confronted with irrefutable evidence of the afterlife, we will have to deal with it whether it suits us or not.

Most of the research into spirit communications has been stimulated by personal need, such as someone losing a loved one. Grief is a powerful motivator. Death will always be a part of the life journey on this planet, and so we will constantly be influenced by it to find ways to reach through that barrier.

15

Into the Future

Someday I hope that my cell phone calling plan will include the afterlife. And maybe a few dimensions beyond that. There are a few people I'd like to check up on and some words of wisdom I'd like to get from higher sources. Wouldn't it be amazing if we could patch in heaven on *Coast to Coast AM*? Now *that* would be a riveting show!

How about television talk shows with the dead? The Internet and instant global telecommunications have turned the planet into a virtual community. We can hook up sound and image among people stretching around the globe. The next step will be interdimensional. Live footage beamed straight into your living room from the astral plane and beyond!

Think of the possibilities of a link to the afterlife. Perhaps you could keep your job on the Other Side in a new version of telecommuting. You could participate in family gatherings and special occasions. Murders, mysterious disappearances, crimes, and accidents could be solved with missing testimonies. Ideas, inspirations, and inventions could be transmitted to the living in a faster and clearer way. And perhaps those on the Other Side could see beyond the curve of the time horizon to give advice on events shaping up in the future.

There is no doubt about it, reliable communication with the dead and spirits could radically change life on earth. Ultimately, things will change for the better—but not without a lot of turmoil first. The lifting of the veil between worlds will not automatically usher in an age of peace, enlightenment, and brotherhood, such as envisioned by some of the EVP pioneers. Many people on this side will not be happy, because some of their fundamental institutions and beliefs will be shaken to the core.

What will happen when that day comes? First, we will have to overcome a tremendous upheaval in science and religion, probably more so in religion than in science. Perhaps by the time we can establish provable communication science will have caught up to the dynamics of the communication itself. Religion is another matter. In spite of the common ground shared by religions about morals, ethics, enlightenment, and so on, religion has divided people over history, not united them. Religions have emphatic things to say about what happens in the afterlife. Irrefutable facts about death and the afterlife will seriously challenge many religious teachings and beliefs. Religious authorities who are accustomed to wielding power and influence over people and nations may find themselves without an audience, which could have dangerous consequences. Too many wars have been waged on Earth over religious views.

Human beings are territorial, too. Will we fight over territorial rights in the afterlife? Technology secrets to be mined in the afterlife? What's more, will we try to *invade* the afterlife? On the heels of communication could come attempts to open another kind of doorway, one that would allow us physical or semi-physical access back and forth. If we master out-of-body projection, will we build armies of astral warriors? *Would we even wage war on the dead?* It may sound far-fetched, but we have to think of all possibilities.

As a Catholic theologian and an EVP researcher, Fr. François Brune anticipated that Electronic Voice Phenomena will reinforce religious faith and that "man will rediscover the reason for his existence—his place in God's plan." That, of course, assumes that EVP evidence will not contradict religious beliefs.

Friedrich Jürgenson believed that the public will have to be:

> confronted gradually with the undeniable facts . . .
> we will have to change our way of thinking from the

bottom up. Many attitudes of thought and feeling will have to disappear. It will take much time and cause much resistance, but in the end the grave will lose its macabre character. If you can hear the living voices of the dead at home, who will want to put on black mourning clothes to visit them in the cemeteries?

Similar scenarios about the need for gradual assimilation have been put forward concerning proof of extraterrestrial life. The scientists who pioneered the SETI program, which searched the radio waves for intelligent signals from outer space, addressed the potential effects of contact. What they had to say about meeting ETs applies equally well to meeting the dead in the afterlife and the nonphysical beings who work with them. While most of the SETI scientists acknowledged some of the same hazards we have just described, they thought the long-term effects of contact would be positive. Astronomer Frank D. Drake stated in an interview in *SETI Pioneers* (1990):

> I don't think it [contact] will lead to catastrophes like the War of the Worlds broadcast, and the real impact will be seen only years later, as the information gathered starts to affect decisions made on Earth, regarding technology, or whatever is affected by the information which is gathered from another civilization. . . .
> [. . . I]t will affect the course of economic de-

velopment, governmental systems, how we cope with population growth, energy and resources—all those things will be affected. And this will have an enormous impact on the nature of the life of human beings.

The astronomer Carl Sagan wrote a best-selling novel on the subject, *Contact* (1985), which was made into a film in 1997, starring Jodie Foster and Matthew McConaughey. In an interview in *SETI Pioneers*, Sagan predicted that public reaction will be "very complex":

Some people will be absolutely delighted and others will be extremely fearful and threatened by it. You'll have involvement of every sector of opinion on the planet. Certainly religious people will be heavily involved in the discussion of what this means and what to do about it. I believe it will have political, social, academic, intellectual implications.

In the long run, Sagan said, the differences that divide us will become insignificant in the face of what humanity faces as a whole.

We can apply all of these thoughts to proof of the afterlife as well. Eventually, we will come up with the hard proof of survival after death—and then we will be in for a roller-coaster ride. I'm an eternal optimist, however. I have a deep belief in the ability of human beings to rise to any challenge and make the best of it. In spite of our troubles throughout history, we have made stunning advancements in all areas of life. When we come face-to-face with the afterlife—while we are still in this life—we will let go of what no longer works and re-create our reality. I know many of my listeners share this attitude, too. *Coast to Coast* is host to the full range of beliefs from doomsday to salvation. Even when we delve into the dark and pessimistic scenarios, we still want to know: how do we make the best of what is to come?

It is crucial that our leaders in science, religion, academia, and even politics pay attention to the research being done in spirit communications in order to be prepared to address the proof when it comes.

DEATH, LIFE, AND REBIRTH

Proof of the afterlife and communication with the Other Side will give us new knowledge of the process of dying and the transition to a new state of being. Redefining death will lead to a redefining of life. We will alter choices we make about how we live life.

We will learn the truth about reincarnation. Most of the people on Earth believe in some form of physical reincarnation or rebirth, despite what some major religions have to say on the topic. Many spirit communicators attest to the reality of reincarnation. Spirit communications could shed light on past lives—or "other" lives, as some prefer, for they may be happening simultaneously in different realities.

Thousands of cases of reincarnation have been researched and documented, and as with spirit communications, the evidence is compelling but not proven scientifically. Yet countless people have an inkling or a deep intuitive feeling that they have lived before, including impressions of certain time periods, places, and even personalities.

Electronic Voice Phenomena made Sarah Estep not only a believer in survival and an afterlife but also a believer in reincarnation. "I know I have lived in this world many, many times," she told Rosemary. After becoming active in spirit communications, Estep made three trips to Egypt, certain she had lived there long ago as other personalities, as long as two thousand years ago. She taped some of her most startling Electronic Voice Phenomena, messages that indicated she had indeed lived in Egypt in ancient times. Estep taped everywhere she went and collected about one hundred messages, half of which were Class A. At a desert site of thousands of Coptic tombs, she walked around, stopping at various tombs and inviting someone to speak. At one tomb, a female voice told her, "I buried you." Estep took a photo of the tomb and in the ensuing years often wondered if she had been buried right there. She had the deep feeling that she had lived several times in ancient Egypt.

She had a moving experience at a small tomb by the pyramids at Giza. She sat on a stone floor by a statue of a small boy and inexplicably became overwhelmed with grief. She taped many messages, including one that said, "I'm back with you." Estep's daughter, Becky, taped as well and got the message "My mother." The voice sounded as though it belonged to an adolescent boy. They wondered if Estep had once been related to the boy of the statue.

Estep was called by name inside the Great Pyramid at Giza. There she also recorded a conversation among communicators about her. A voice asked if she could be trusted, and another voice answered, "Yes, she is a good person."

Rosemary has been working with Paul von Ward, a researcher into reincarnation and consciousness, to devise some real-time EVP experiments that could validate past lives. Von Ward focuses on the psychophysical evidence for past lives found in a person's physical traits, career choices, innate skills, interests, and so on, which he discusses in his book *The Soul Genome: Science and Reincarnation* (2008). The experiments involve blind questions. Who knows where the answers will come from—the dead, other entities, or perhaps even our parallel selves.

PERSONAL CHANGES

Equally significant to institutional revolution are changes that will affect us individually as well as collectively. Spirit communications are likely to enhance our natural psychic and intuitive abilities. At some point, we may not need equipment at all to contact the dead—we may be able to do it mentally, much like a medium.

Enhanced psychic ability means that our own thoughts will be more transparent to more living people, too. It will be harder to hide evil, manipulative, deceitful thoughts—people will be caught "thought naked."

Imagine what it would be like to hear everyone's honest, unvarnished thoughts. We would literally have to retrain the way we think. Would we learn another way to mask dishonesty? Or would we purify ourselves of deceit?

If we take the high road, changes in our consciousness will exert significant changes in our physical form. In all of our mystical philosophies, as we become more enlightened our physical form changes into more of a "light body." Author Michael Murphy mapped out these changes in his groundbreaking work *The Future of the Body* (1992). The "superhuman" of the future will have enhanced consciousness, abilities we now consider to be paranormal, and a different body as a result of the first two:

- Extraordinary perceptions in the form of psi.
- Extraordinary somatic (related to the body) awareness and self-regulation.
- Extraordinary communication abilities, such as telepathy, and ecstatic states.
- Superabundant vitality beyond ordinary body processes.
- Extraordinary movement abilities.
- Extraordinary capacities to alter the environment, such as through psychokinesis (mind over matter).
- Self-existent delight.
- Supreme intellectual capacities and genius abilities.
- Volition exceeding ordinary will, producing extraordinary actions.

• Transcendent personhood.
• Transcendent love.
• Alterations in bodily structures, states, and processes.

Science has already documented the power of the mind in healing—positive thought, intention, prayer, visualization, and so on. "That we can creatively alter our muscles, organs, cells and molecular processes is clearly established," said Murphy. "Given that fact, we can wonder about the limits of self-induced bodily change. Might our bodies accommodate alterations beyond those presently mapped by medical science?"

These changes are not likely to happen overnight but probably will progress over a long period of time. We are likely to be advised and guided by spirit communicators in the process.

Above all, we have to make the *choice* to explore the territory. The spirit communicators have emphasized that the interdimensional bridge will truly happen only when we bring the right intentions to it. The devices we use may become less important than the thoughts, intentions, and motivations we have behind them.

In my book *Journey to the Light*, I talked about my "conspiracy theory." Simply stated, it is that all things are possible when we open ourselves up to messages from the great universe. This involves not only intuition and inspiration but also signals from other intelligences. Our playing field is vast, including not only the Earth but also the afterlife, other worlds, and other dimensions. As I also noted in *Journey to the Light*, there are forces and people right here, right now, that wish to see humanity spiritually enslaved and limited in order to perpetuate their own interests and control. The only way we will break out of that is to push forward and be willing to embrace bold new revelations and ideas.

We do not die. Beyond the threshold of physical life lies limitless potential of thought, existence, and realization. That is our true destiny, and we must reach for it without hesitation.

Experimenting on Your Own

I f you haven't already tried spirit communications, you
are probably inspired to do so now, so we'd like to re-
mind you of a few pointers that we have discussed in this
book. Here are nine tips to always keep in mind.

First and foremost, establish a regular spiritual practice.
Even a few minutes a day of meditation or prayer can re-
orient your spiritual compass and keep your thoughts and
intention on a higher level. Meditation in particular opens
and refines the third-eye faculty, the ability to discern the
spiritual realms.

Second, expect good results. We have noted that some of
the leading and most successful researchers got started

because of their doubt and skepticism—but as they got deeper into the work, they became convinced that those who are open to results and *expect* to get them ultimately have the highest success rate. Everyone in the field knows individuals who contradict the "ideal model" and still get good results, of course. But why not get the odds going as best as possible in your favor?

Many researchers find that establishing a regular schedule of experimentation helps, too, especially in the beginning. There may be a conditioning factor at work. Rosemary keeps no regular schedule with her experiments. You just have to try different approaches until you find what works best for you.

Third, experiment with different techniques and equipment. Again, there is no "best" setup for everyone. Spirit communications are highly individualistic. Eventually you will find the equipment and methods that work best for you.

Fourth, keep sessions short. Long recording sessions tend to be counterproductive. Traditional EVP results can be obtained with just five to ten minutes of recording time. For radio sweep devices, there seems to be a window of peak contact. It takes an average of five to ten minutes for the equipment to warm up, followed by a peak window for communications that lasts for about thirty to forty-five minutes. The energy then drops. Some sessions can go longer, of course—and some will be shorter. With practice, you develop a sense of how well it's working.

Fifth, be respectful to the communicators. The so-called

"reality" television programs often show ghost hunters screaming at the "ghosts" to perform for them. If in fact the "ghosts" are remnants of deceased human beings, why would you be rude to them? Would you be similarly rude to living people? Would *you* want to cooperate with someone who was abusive to you? Provocation may make for television entertainment, but it is ineffective for research.

Alexander MacRae, a Scottish EVP researcher, had encounters that influenced him in how to address spirits; evidently, he needed to be more polite himself. Once when he was conducting experiments with an international team to investigate whether or not EVP utterances could be related to the questions posed by the experimenter, MacRae devised a list of six standard questions, to be asked with thirty seconds between each question.

In one round, MacRae asked, "What is your name?"

In answer, he got a voice that sounded like Top Cat, a streetwise cartoon character with a New York accent: "Who wantsa know?"

In another round, MacRae asked the same question, only to be answered by a gruff voice that said, "Stop shovin' me around."

Wondering what was going on, MacRae then realized that he probably sounded as though he were conducting an interrogation, not a conversation. He changed the question to, "Would you mind telling me your name?" Responses were better and more in context to the questions. Interestingly, as time went by responses related less to the questions he asked and more to other communicators, as though the living became eavesdroppers on conversations held by the discarnate. Evidently our Electronic Voice Phenomena make connections among the communicators as well.

Sometimes communicators are rude. If they will not stop on request, turn your recorders or devices off.

Sixth, avoid excessive software manipulation of audio files. You may create Electronic Voice Phenomena that don't exist.

Seventh, get the opinions of others in evaluating your results. The best communications are the clearest.

Eighth, join discussion forums and groups. An exchange of ideas and results will not only help your progress, but help the research of others as well.

Ninth, be persistent. Results may not come immediately, especially for beginners. Here again, television can be misleading. For the sake of entertainment, television ghost hunters get results every time. Not so in the real world of paranormal research. Sometimes you may get a lot, sometimes very little, sometimes nothing noteworthy at all. Some of the leading researchers tried for weeks, without success, in their beginnings. Once the link forms, communication becomes much easier. Keep at it, even if results are not as grand as you would wish. You never know when a big breakthrough may come—and you may be the person getting it. Good luck, and let us know how you fare.

Bibliography

Bander, Peter. *Voices from the Tapes: Recording from the Other World.* New York: Drake Publishers, 1973.

———. *Carry on Talking: How Dead Are the Voices?* Gerrards Cross, England: Colin Smythe, 1972.

Berger, Arthur S. *Evidence of Life After Death: A Casebook for the Tough-Minded.* Springfield, Ill.: Charles C Thomas, 1988.

———. *Aristocracy of the Dead.* Jefferson, N.C.: McFarland, 1987.

Butler, Tom F., and Lisa W. *There Is No Death and There Are No Dead: Evidence of Survival and Spirit Communication*

Through Voices and Images from Those on the Other Side. Reno, Nev.: AA-EVP, 2003.

Cardoso, Anabela. *Electronic Voices: Contact with Another Dimension?* Ropley, England: O Books, 2010.

Cheney, Margaret. *Tesla: Man Out of Time.* New York: Touchstone, 2001.

Copeland, Martha. *I'm Still Here.* Reno, Nev.: AA-EVP, 2005.

Estep, Sarah. *Roads to Eternity.* Lakeville, Minn.: Galde Press, 2005.

————. *Voices of Eternity.* New York: Fawcett, 1988.

Fontana, David. *Life Beyond Death: What Should We Expect?* London: Watkins, 2009.

Fuller, John G. *The Ghost of 29 Megacycles.* New York: Signet/New American Library, 1981.

Jürgenson, Friedrich. *Voice Transmissions with the Deceased.* Friedrich Jürgenson Foundation: http://www.fargfab riken.se/fjf/.

Kraasa, Peter. *Father Ernetti's Chronovisor: The Creation and Disappearance of the World's First Time Machine.* New York: New Paradigm Books, 2000.

Locher, Theo, and Maggie Harsch-Fischbach. *Breakthroughs in Technical Spirit Communication.* Boulder, Colo.: Continuing Life Research, 1997.

MacRae, Alexander. *EVP and New Dimensions.* Lulu.com, 2004.

Macy, Mark. *The Project.* New York: Eloquent Books, 2009.

————. *Spirit Faces: Truth About the Afterlife.* York Beach, Maine: Red Wheel/Weiser Books, 2006.

———. *Miracles in the Storm: Talking to the Other Side with the New Technology of Spiritual Contact.* New York: New American Library, 2001.

Meek, George. *Enjoy Your Own Funeral: And Live a Happy Forever.* Lakeville, Minn.: Galde Press, 1999.

———. *After We Die, What Then?* Columbus, Ohio: Ariel Press, 1987.

Raudive, Konstantin. *Breakthrough: An Amazing Experiment in Electronic Communication with the Dead.* New York: Taplinger, 1971.

Rogo, Scott, and Raymond Bayless. *Phone Calls from the Dead.* Englewood Cliffs, N.J.: Prentice-Hall, 1979.

Rountree, David M. *Paranormal Technology: Understanding the Science of Ghost Hunting.* iUniverse.com, 2010.

Schwartz, Gary E. with William Simon. *The Afterlife Experiments: Breakthrough Scientific Evidence of Life After Death.* New York: Atria Books, 2003.

Senkowski, Ernst. *Instrumental Transcommunication.* World ITC: http://www.worlditc.org, 1995.

Smith, Susy. *The Afterlife Codes: Searching for Evidence of Survival of the Soul.* Charlottesville, Va.: Hampton Roads Publishing, 2000.

———. *Voices of the Dead—Radio Broadcast, Psychokinetic Power—Or Messages from Beyond the Grave . . . ?* Bergenfield, N.J.: The New American Library, 1977.

Swedenborg, Emanuel. *Heaven and Hell.* Translated by George F. Dole. New York: Swedenborg Foundation, 1976.

Van Praagh, James. *Talking to Heaven: A Medium's Message of Life After Death.* New York: Dutton Publishers, 1997.

Weisberg, Barbara. *Talking to the Dead: Kate and Maggie Fox and the Rise of Spiritualism.* San Francisco: Harper-SanFrancisco, 2004.